George, Bishop of the Arabs: Homily on the Consecration of Myron

Texts from Christian Late Antiquity

60

Series Editor

George Anton Kiraz

TeCLA (Texts from Christian Late Antiquity) is a series presenting ancient Christian texts both in their original languages and with accompanying contemporary English translations.

George, Bishop of the Arabs: Homily on the Consecration of Myron

Translated by

Baby Varghese

Appendix by Sebastian P. Brock

2020

Gorgias Press LLC, 954 River Road, Piscataway, NJ, 08854, USA

www.gorgiaspress.com

Copyright © 2020 by Gorgias Press LLC

All rights reserved under International and Pan-American Copyright Conventions. No part of this publication may be reproduced, stored in a retrieval system or transmitted in any form or by any means, electronic, mechanical, photocopying, recording, scanning or otherwise without the prior written permission of Gorgias Press LLC.

2020

ISBN 978-1-4632-0731-1   **ISSN 1935-6846**

Library of Congress Cataloging-in-Publication Data

A Cataloging-in-Publication Record is available from the Library of Congress.

Printed in the United States of America

TABLE OF CONTENTS

Table of Contents v
Introduction 1
    Metrical Homily on the Consecration of Myron 3
    Liturgical Rites 6
    The Present Edition 7
    Bibliography and Abbreviations 8
Text and Translation 13
Appendix 91
    By Sebastian Brock
Index of Biblical References 99
Index of Names 101

INTRODUCTION

George was one of the last scholarly Syrian Orthodox bishops to live in the early Islamic period. Very little is known about his life.[1] He was probably from the area around Antioch, perhaps from Guma and was born ca. 660 (not 640 as Ryssel suggests).[2] After completing his early education under the local clergy, he seems to have studied at the famous monastic school of Qennesrin on the banks of Euphrates, perhaps the most important center of Greek studies in the Syrian Orthodox Church of the 7th and 8th centuries. George was probably an associate of Jacob of Edessa, who was in Qennesrin for some time. They were contemporaries and were from the same region.[3] His studies at Qennesrin helped him to acquire a respectable knowledge of Greek language, science and Aristotle's philosophy and especially to be promoted as bishop. Thus he translated the works of Aristotle into Syriac (*The Organon*) and completed the *Hexameron* (= Discourse on the Six Days of Creation) of his friend Jacob of Edessa which had been left incomplete at Jacob's death in 708.

According to Michel the Syrian, just before his death, Patriarch Athanasius II of Balad ordered his Metropolitan Sergius Zukunaya to ordain George as bishop of the Christian Arab Tribes (or 'nations' – *ammē*) of the Hyrta region, under the Maphrianate of Tagrit. The Arab tribes *'Aqulaye, Tu'yaye* and *Tanukaye* were under his pastoral care.[4] We can assume that he probably knew Arabic as

---

[1] On his life see TANNOUS, pp. 672–679. See also BROCK, *Pseudo- Dionysius*.
[2] TANNOUS, p. 675.
[3] Ibid.
[4] Ibid. p. 709.

well. Tannous has remarked that George was 'bilingual', perhaps 'trilingual'.[5] He also compiled a large number of *Scholia* on the homilies of Gregory of Nazianzus which shows that he had read extensively. George's commentary on the scriptures, in the form of *Scholia*, has been cited in the Catena of the Monk Severus and by Bar Hebraeus in *Ausar Roze* (= *The Storehouse of Mysteries*).

An exposition of the mysteries of *Baptism, Eucharist and Myron* attributed to George has been published by R.H. Connolly.[6] He was a gifted poet and authored six long homilies in twelve syllables: a homily on the Holy Myron in two recensions, a treatise on the Calendar,[7] a homily on Severus of Antioch,[8] a homily on the feast of Hosanna,[9] and a homily on the Forty Martyrs of Sebaste. A *Sugitho* (canticle) in heptasyllabic meter on Abraham and his Sacrifice is also known under his name.[10] He carried on extensive correspondences (preserved in BL 12154, fol. 222–291).[11] The most important among them is that written to the priest and recluse Yeshu of Innib (north of Aleppo), in which George refers to Aphrahat and his works.

George wrote a longer and shorter homily on Myron in twelve-syllable meter. V. Ryssel translated both of them into German.[12] In 1892, Ryssel edited the longer version,[13] sometimes attributed to Jacob of Serugh. This is because Jacob usually wrote in this meter and it is popularly known as the meter of Jacob. The shorter version has now been edited by Sebastian P. Brock.[14]

---

[5] Ibid. 712–13.
[6] George, *Com.*
[7] J. S. Assemani, *Bibliotheca Orientalis* [2 Vols. Rome, 1719–1721] I, 495.
[8] McVey, *George*.
[9] Rillet, *Hom*. Tannous, McVey and Rillet give introduction to the works of George.
[10] See Barsoum p. 117; on the mss. Ibid. p. 218, n. 471 ff. On the other works of George, see Barsoum. Ibid. and Tannous.
[11] On the topics of his letters, see Tannous.
[12] Ryssel, *Gedichte*. Longer version: pp. 14–36; 156–163; Shorter version pp. 9–14; 155–156.
[13] Ryssel, pp. 46–80.
[14] Brock, *Bishop*.

METRICAL HOMILY ON THE CONSECRATION OF MYRON

The Syrian Orthodox Church gives special importance to the Holy Myron, used for the post baptismal Chrismation, consecration of the baptismal water as well as for the consecration of the churches and *Tablaitho* (Antimension). The interest of the Syrian Orthodox Church in the 'mystery' of Holy Myron is a tradition that goes back to the *Ecclesiastical Hierarchy* (ch. 4) of Pseudo-Dionysius Areopagite (c.500). In fact, the works of Dionysius were translated into Syriac in the early decades of the sixth century and were revised and commented upon by Syriac writers.[15] Following the approach of Dionysius, Syrian Orthodox writers gave attention to both the celebration and the meaning of the consecration of Holy Myron.

Nine treatises on the Consecration of Myron have come down to us: (1) by Patriarch John I of Antioch (d. 648); (2) by Jacob of Edessa (d. 708); (3) – (4) by George Bishop of the Arabs (one brief prose commentary and a long Metrical homily published here); (5) by Moses bar Kepha (d.903); (6) by Antony of Tagrit (9th century); (7) by Lazar Bar Sabta (9th cent: lost ?); (8) by Dionysius Bar Salibi (d. 1171); and (9) by Bar Hebraeus (d. 1286) – *Mnarat Kudshe*: sixth base (a summary is given in *Zalge*). All except the Treatise of Antony of Tagrit have been published.[16]

Among various Syriac treatise on Myron, the homily by George, published here, is the only one in verse. Homilies of the patriarch John and Jacob of Edessa were certainly preached during the consecration. Sometimes they were paraphrased or new homilies were composed on their model *(see bibliography)*. The works of Antony of Tagrit, Bar Kepha and Bar Salibi were rather commentaries in the strict sense.

The metrical homily of George was probably composed to be sung during the consecration of the Myron. The style is reminiscent of that of St Ephrem and Jacob of Serugh. The author follows an

---

[15] See BROCK, *Pseudo- Dionysius* pp. 128–129.
See also STROTHMANN, *Das Sakrament der Myron-Weihe* pp. 1–2 (gives both Syriac version of Sergius of Resh'ayna (d.536) and Phokas of Edessa (late 7th cent).
Also ID, "Pseudo-Dionysios Areopagita", 188–196.
[16] See the bibliography.

allegorical exegetical method with occasional use of typology. It is not a systematic commentary on the rite of consecration, like those of Moses Bar Kepha or Dionysius Bar Salibi. The author makes only a few allusions to the rites as such. There are striking difference between the 'Exposition of the mysteries' (published by R.H. Connolly) and the metrical homily. Though one can argue that the two works are not by the same author, we cannot exclude the possibility that the two works represent two stages in the literary career of the same author and were composed for two different purposes. The homily was probably composed for liturgical use (which perhaps explains the origin of two versions of the metrical homily), whereas the Exposition was addressed to the ordinary clergy and faithful (perhaps even the summary of a larger treatise).

The metrical homily attests that George was a gifted poet and a theologian who could articulate his thought with remarkable lucidity. He draws on biblical exegesis as well as on the Christological issues debated during his day. In his metrical homily, George explains the 'meaning of the oil and the anointing' in terms of the mystery of Christ.

In the early Syriac tradition, attested since the days of St Ephrem (d. 373), oil is a symbol of Christ.[17] Thus in his *Hymn on Virginity* (IV,7), St Ephrem writes: "The name of oil ... is like a Symbol and in it is portrayed the name of the Anointed (*msiho*)".[18] In this stanza, St Ephrem plays on the words *msh* (anoint), oil (*mesho*) and *msiho* (Messiah). On the other hand, the patristic tradition saw a messianic prophecy in the Song of Songs (1:3): "Your name is oil poured out/emptied out". The Septuagint rendering is "Your name is the Myron poured/emptied out", whose Syriac translation is regularly quoted by Syriac fathers like Patriarch John (Myron, # 8) or Jacob of Edessa (Myron # 7).[19] Following these lines, George uses a series of titles for Christ. Christ is called "Pure Myron" (line 1); "Aromatic oil" (l.3); "Fine Nard" (l.5) and "oil of holiness" (l.25). Christ is the "pure myrrh" (l. 92; cfr. Songs 1:13).

---

[17] See B. VARGHESE, *Onctions...* pp. 47–49.
[18] K. MCVEY (tr), *Ephrem, Hymns*, p. 277.
[19] On the origin of this rendering see, BROCK, *Jacob of Edessa, Myron*, p. 31, n. 63).

Jacob of Edessa speaks of the "emptying out of the Son of God: "'Emptied out' because, being full and overflowing, he emptied himself into our human form and made our wretched and feeble race full and no longer deficient".[20]

This is certainly based on the Pauline theology of "the self-emptying (*kenosis*) of Christ" (Phil. 2:7). George explains the emptying out in terms of the theology of deification, as articulated by St Athanasius:

> " Oh Son of God, who of Your own sanctified Yourself;
> And became man to make men gods" (l. 57–58).

George shows how the entire earthly life of Christ was an example of his humility, that is, his self-emptying (l. 107–114).

George duly explains the miaphysite Christology ("One incarnate Nature of Christ") as followed by the Syrian Orthodox tradition. He duly underscores the reality of the human nature of Christ. According to him, in the Upper room, the risen Christ showed his wounds to his disciples to "drive away the phantasy of the Phantasiasts" (those who held that the humanity of Christ was not real, but only an appearance). (cfr. l. 117–118). Christ appeared to his disciples in a room that was shut in order to show that as "God he can pass through solid objects" (l. 115–116).

Christ has done everything for our salvation. He is present in the sacraments and the liturgical celebrations and we converse with him and he cherishes us (l. 130). Liturgical celebrations are means to convince us of the reality of what he has done for humanity (l. 132), as well as of his promises (l. 133). They proclaim and convince us of the reality of the divinity and humanity of Christ (l. 134).

George's audience was certainly aware of the Christological controversies of the day. Like his predecessors such as Severus of Antioch and Philoxenus of Mabbugh, George regarded "Nestorians" and "Chalcedonians" as those who "divide the Son of God" (l. 170). Following the Alexandrian Christology as expounded by Cyril of Alexandria, Syrian Orthodox fathers give emphasis to the divine nature of Christ ("Christology from above"). Christ is above

---

[20] Jacob of Edessa, *Myron* #7.

all God incarnate and is "A True One from the True One without division" (l. 135). "While remaining God, in His love, he became man" (l. 137). He was God even when He suffered human limitations (l. 139). But in no way do George and the Syriac fathers minimize the human nature. "Also (He was) man, when He did the divine deeds" (l.140). George speaks of Christ as "Son of God who became Christ with humanity" (l.148).

In the anointing or in baptism, we put on Christ (l. 180; 183–184). In bread and in wine, we receive Him (l. 181). As we have mentioned above, George's style is direct and lucid. Thus he presents the goal of incarnation in terms of renewal (l. 185–189).

LITURGICAL RITES

The following is an outline of the liturgy of the Consecration of Myron.[21]

- Maundy Thursday third hour, the singers are grouped in three choirs.
- Hymns; Sedro; censing of the nave by the bishop; OT lessons.
- Bishop enters the sanctuary and mixes the balsam oil with perfumed olive oil.
- Solemn Procession with the bottle of Myron in the nave; 12 priests, 12 deacons and 12 sub-deacons accompany with censors, fans and lights.
- Consecration (structure similar to that of anaphora).
- Signing crosses over the bottle and Epiclesis.
- Exaltation of the bottle on Bema.
- Concludes with a homily, and deacon's litany.

George does not refer to every element of the service. His comments are limited to the most important ones. According to the homily, the consecration of Myron took place on Maundy Thursday (l.203–204), a custom that existed until the days of Bar Hebraeus (13th cent). It was held at the third hour (l.215–16). The cer-

---

[21] For the detailed outline see, *Nomocanon* 3:4; (tr). VARGHESE, pp. 50–53; BEDJAN, pp. 31–34; Bar Kepha, *Myron*, p. viii.

emony was presided over by the bishop, dressed in white garments (l. 319), the usual colour for festal celebrations in the Syrian Orthodox Church until the Late Middle Ages. The bishop enters the sanctuary and mixes olive oil and Balsam, which symbolizes "the union of divinity and humanity" (l. 325–328).

The procession with the bottle of Myron, reminiscent of the Pre-anaphoral offertory procession, was the most solemn part of the celebration. Thus George offers a long commentary on it (l. 345–416). The procession leaves the sanctuary and moves to the northern side of the church, and goes in an anti-clockwise direction, reaches south and returns to the sanctuary and the bishop then places the bottle on the altar. North to South movement is given an allegorical interpretation (l. 379–404). The consecration is completed with an epiclesis (l. 425–434), signing of the crosses over the holy oil (l. 453–54), followed by the exaltation of the bottle on the bema in the middle of the nave towards four sides (l. 455–469). George points out that the oil is used primarily in the baptismal anointing (l. 521–524). It is not clear whether Myron was used for the consecration of the church in his day.

Most of the ideas that George expounds are already found in the homilies of Patriarch John and Jacob of Edessa. The metrical homily of George is primarily a liturgical hymn, though a few lines are dedicated to explain the miaphysite doctrine of Christ.

The homily of the Patriarch John is more biblical and pastoral. He dwells on the Old Testament figures of the oil and their fulfillment in the holy oil. John makes practically no reference to the liturgy, except that it was held "once a year" (# 12) and some remarks on the Procession (# 13).

THE PRESENT EDITION

As we have noted above, George composed a longer and shorter version of the homily on the Consecration of Myron. The longer version edited by Ryssel (in 1892) is reproduced here, as the Syriac text is not always accessible to the students of Syriac language and liturgy. I have published an English translation in *The Harp* (Vol. 12, 2006, pp. 255–282). Here, I give a revised translation which was corrected by Dr. Sebastian Brock. Dr. Brock has also prepared detailed notes on the variant textual readings, given in an appendix. I am grateful to Dr. Brock for his kindness and willingness to read my translations into English, a language which is not my mother tongue. I am solely responsible for any errors or printing mistakes in the Syriac or English text that remain. My sincere thanks to my friend Dr. George Kiraz for accepting the text for publication and also to Dr. Melonie Schmierer-Lee, who with her commendable skills edited the text.

BIBLIOGRAPHY AND ABBREVIATIONS

Antony of Tagrit (c.830/50), *Treatise on the Myron*, BL Add. 14726, fol. 72r–85r.

Bar Hebraeus, *Nomocanon*	Bedjan, P., *Nomocanon Gregori Barhebraei*, Paris,1898. [English Translation of the first eight chapters: B. Varghese, *Book of Guides (Hudaya) or Nomocanon: Gregorios Bar Hebraeus*, MOC Publications, Kottayam, 2014].
Bar Hebraeus, *Mnarat Kudshe*	B. Varghese (Syr. & Eng), "Bar Hebraeus: Mnarat Qudshe: Sixth Base on Earthly Priesthood", *The Harp* 30 (2016), pp. 147–229.
Bar Kepha, *Myron*	B. Varghese (Syr. & Eng), *Moses Bar Kepha: Commentary on Myron*, Gorgias Press, Texts from Christian Antiquity 34, Piscataway, NJ, 2014. (see also Strothmann)
Bar Salibi, *Myron*	B. Varghese (Syr. & Eng), *Dionysius Bar Salibi: Commentary on Myron and Baptism*, Moran 'Etho 29, SEERI, Kottayam, 2006.
BARSOUM	Patriarch Ignatius Aphraim I Barsoum, *The History of Syriac Literature and Sciences*, (tr. By Matti Moosa), Passeggiata Press, Pueblo, 2000.
BROCK, *Pseudo-Dionysius*	Sebastian P. Brock, "Dionysius the Areopagite, Pseudo", in Sebastian P. Brock et als, (ed), *Gorgias Encyclopedic Dictionary of the Syriac Heritage*, Gorgias Press, Piscataway, NJ, 2011, pp. 128–129.

BROCK, *George*	ID., Giwargi, bishop of the Arab Tribes", ID. pp. 177–178.
BROCK, *Bishop*	Sebastian P. Brock, "George, Bishop of the Arab Tribes, mimro on the Myron (BL Add. 12,165)', *Syrian Orthodox Patriarchal Journal* 56 (2018), 1–28.
Dionysius, *HE*	Dionysius the Areopagite, *The Ecclesiastical Hierarchy, Patrologia Graeca* III, 369–569. Eng.tr. Colm Luibheid, *Pseudo-Dionysius. The Complete Works*, (New York, 1987), 193–259.
George, *Com*.	"An Exposition of the Mysteries of the Church made by a certain bishop George, in Connolly, R.H., & H.W. Codrington, (ed. & tr) *Two Commentaries on the Jacobite Liturgy by George, Bishop of the Arab Tribes and Moses bar Kepha....,* Oxford, 1913, pp. 11–23 (Eng.tr).
Jacob of Edessa, *Myron*	S. Brock (ed), "Jacob of Edessa's Discourse on the Myron", *Oriens Christianus* 63 (1979), pp. 20–36.
John I, *Myron*	B. Varghese (tr), "John, Patriarch of Antioch: Homily on the Consecration of Myron", *The Harp* 24 (2012), 157–166. [Syriac text published by Martikainen, pp. 169–209].
MCVEY, *Ephrem, Hymns*	K. McVey, *Ephrem the Syrian. Hymns*, Paulist Press, New York, 1989.
MCVEY, *George*	K. McVey (ed), George, *Bishop of the Arabs. A homily on Blessed Mar Severus, Patriarch of Antioch*, CSCO 531; SS 217, (Louvain, 1993).
MARTIKAINEN, *Johannes*	Juoako Martikainen (ed), *Johannes I Sedra. Einleitung, Syrische Texte, Übersetzungen*, GOFS, Wiesbaden,

	1991 [Syriac Text of *Homily on Myron*, pp. 169–209].
RILLET, *Hom.*	F. Rillet, « Une homélie sut la fête des hosannas attribuée à Georges, évêque des Arabes », *Oriens Christianus* 74 (1990), 72–102.
RYSSEL, *Gedichte*	V. Ryssel, *Georges des Araberbischofs Gedichte und Briefe*, Leipzig, 1891.
ID., *Poemi*	ID., "Poemi siriaci di Giorgio vescovo degli Arabi", *Atti della Reale Accademia dei Lincei, Ser. 4, Classe di scienze morali, storiche e filologiche*, 9 (1892), 46–93 (on Myron).
STROTHMANN, *Moses*	Werner Strothmann (ed.& tr), *Moses Bar Kepha: Myron-Weihe*, Göttinger Orientforschungen, Reihe I, Syriaca [= GOFS], No.7, Wiesbaden, 1973. (Syriac and German Translation).
ID., *Sakrament*	ID. *Das Sakrament der Myron-Weihe in der Schrift de Ecclesiastica Hierarchia des Pseudo-Dionysios Areopagita in syrischen Übersetzungen und Kommentaren* (Teil 1 & 2), GOFS 15, Wissban 1977.
ID. "Ps-Dionysios"	ID. „Pseudo-Dionysios Areopagita und das Sakrament der Myronweihe", *Zeitschrift der deutschen Morgenländischen Gesellschaft*, Suppl. 4 (1980), 188-196.
TANNOUS	Jack Tannous, "Between Christology and Kalam? The Life and Letters of George, Bishop of the Arab Tribes", in George A. Kiraz (ed), *Malphono w-Rabo d-Malphone. Studies in Honor of Sebastian P. Brock*, Gorgias Eastern Christian Studies 3, Gorgias Press, Piscataway, NJ, 2008, pp. 671–716.

VARGHESE, *Onctions*	B. Varghese, *Les onctions baptismales dans la tradition syrienne,* CSCO 512, Subsidia 82, Louvain, 1989.
VARGHESE, "George"	ID. "George, bishop of the Arabs. Homily on the Consecration of Myron", *The Harp* 19 (2006), 255–280.
VOSTE, *Pontificale*	J.-M Voste (tr), *Pontificale iuxta ritum Ecclesiae Syrorum Occidentalium id est Antionhiae, Pars I, continens consecrationem Myri et Eccleaise,* Versio Latina, S. Congregazione Pro Ecclesia Orientali, Vatican, 1941.

Homilies on the Consecration of Myron [Anonymous]:

Vatican Syr, 51, fol. 20v–24r;

Paris Syr. Fol. 109r sv;

Paris Syr. 60v–65r. [There three homilies are identical].

BL. Add 21210, fol. 202r–205r.

See also VOSTE, *Pontifical*, pp. 44–53.

Text and Translation

George Bishop of the Arabs:
Homily on the Consecration of Myron

1 Pure Myron that filled Your Church with sweet scent,
   Grant to me the sense of smell, so that rejoicingly I may be made fragrant by You.
   Aromatic oil, which was poured out upon humanity,
   With you, may my head be anointed, and may I proclaim on earth the mystery of Your resurrection.
5 Fine nard that has filled the universe with its intensity,[1]
   From You may I acquire a sweet fragrance, and with You, may I sing to You.
   Delightful rose, by whose smell even the dead come to life,
   By You, may my wretched tongue be revived and be refreshed.

   Delightful fruit, that in the Church has become food for us,
10 May the nations that have enjoyed You and consumed You be enriched.
   Choice perfume to which no aroma can be compared,
   With You, may the words of my homily become pleasing in giving praise.

   May Your name be for You the Oil of Myron[2] that pleases you,
   'For Your mercy is better than life'.[3] May I delight in it.
15 Blessed field that Isaac indicated in his prophecy,[4]
   From You, may I gather the sweet-smelling spike of life.

   Choice Censer, who reconciled Your Sender by its fragrance,
   By You, may all my senses take delight in praising You.
   Plant of life that sprouted from the dry earth and ascended,
20 Exhale Your fragrance among the choirs, so that they may praise You.

---

[1] Cant. 1:12; Mk 14:3; Jn 12:3.
[2] Cfr. Cant. 1:3 (LXX).
[3] Ps. 63:3.
[4] Gen. 27:27.

---

[5] Syriac text edited by V. Ryssel, in *Atti della R. Accademia dei Lincei*, IV.9, (Roma 1892), 48–80.

Hidden One, who is hidden from the angels in the heights above,
Reveal in me Your mysteries and may I proclaim on earth to anyone who hears me.

Child of the Father, who became the child of a destitute woman,
Grant me a mind that in silent wonder glorifies You.

25 Oil of holiness that flowed from the source of holiness,
Sanctify my lips that they may praise You in holy fashion.
Son of the Kind One, from whom flow all sorts of delights,
In You, may the soul that desires Your kindness find delight.

Do not, because I have sinned, reject me, O Son of the Merciful One,
30 For You did not reject the harlot who approached You.[6]
With her I press on to narrate Your story, I rejoicing as I do,
For I have seen Your love that flows abundantly even upon the impure.

If I weigh my faults, they will outweigh much more than hers,
Therefore, grant to me even greater mercy than to her!
35 You wish to give absolution and holiness,
For, behold, I see that tax-collectors are also made holy:

However great was the wickedness, it received purity and holiness,
However great was the wound, it received medicaments.
Therefore, in my case, let it not be irksome to You to purify me.
40 And in addition, grant me that I may narrate Your story carefully.

May I become a second Mathew in proclamation,[7]
For my role as a tax-collector is greater than his; (as) in his case, have mercy on me!
It is not that I want to define You, my Lord, for You cannot be defined;
But may I delight in Your praises and also give (others) delight.

---

[6] Cfr. Lk. 7:36–50.
[7] Mt. 9:9.

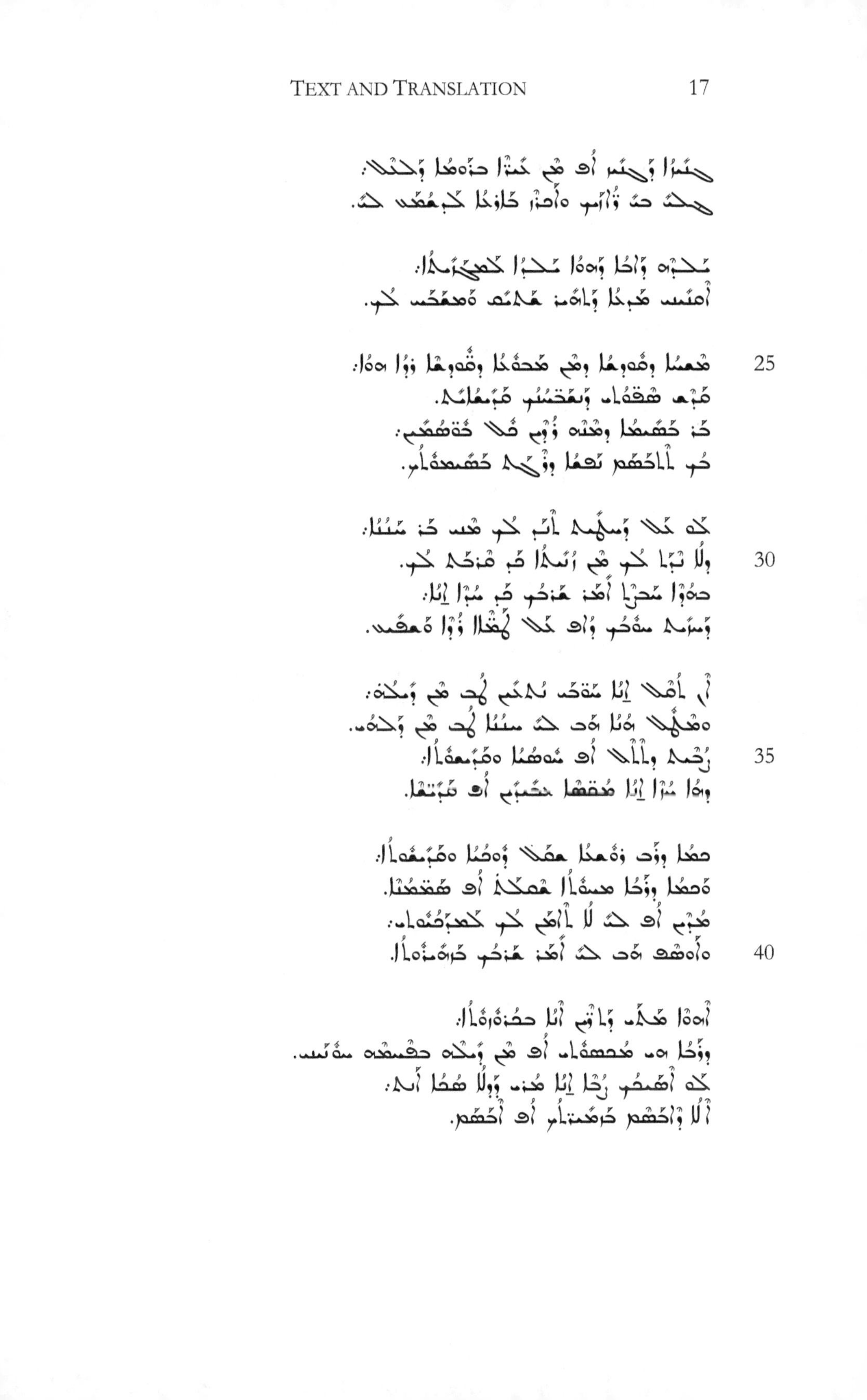

45   Daughter of the Arameans seized hold of me and stopped (me) to ask:
What is the mystery of the unction of the Son of the Holy One?
Therefore, may I be strengthened by You in explaining it,
For its story cannot be told, except with You.

May I become as it were a harp for You, Lord, and speak in me!
50   For great is the mystery and You are holy and I am weak.
'Set now a guard for my mouth',[8] lest it turn aside,
Lest I deal inadequately with (Your) story and become an abuser to the King.

May my voice, the words, and the song become Yours,
And may I become a flute and do You sing in me!
55   In You I trust knowing that I am feeble,
Sanctify my tongue with Your holy songs.

O Son of God who of Your own will sanctified Yourself,
And became man to make men gods.[9]
Grant me that I may speak of Your abasement in wonder,
60   And may the Church rejoice with the assembly of her children as she learns Your mysteries.

O Daughter of the nations, summon the son of Jesse to sing for you,
For that initiate saw your adornment and called you blessed.
'Behold the King's daughter!', he addressed you in his prophecy,
'Who stands in glory at the right hand of the great King'.[10]

65   O impoverished lady, who suddenly became rich with immense wealth!
Daughter of beggars, whom the King betrothed and made His own.
Daughter of the licentious parents, who became chaste and holy,
Daughter of the uneducated, behold, who all of a sudden has become learned.

---

[8] Ps. 141:3.
[9] Cfr. St Athanasius, *On Incarnation*, 54.
[10] Ps. 45:9.

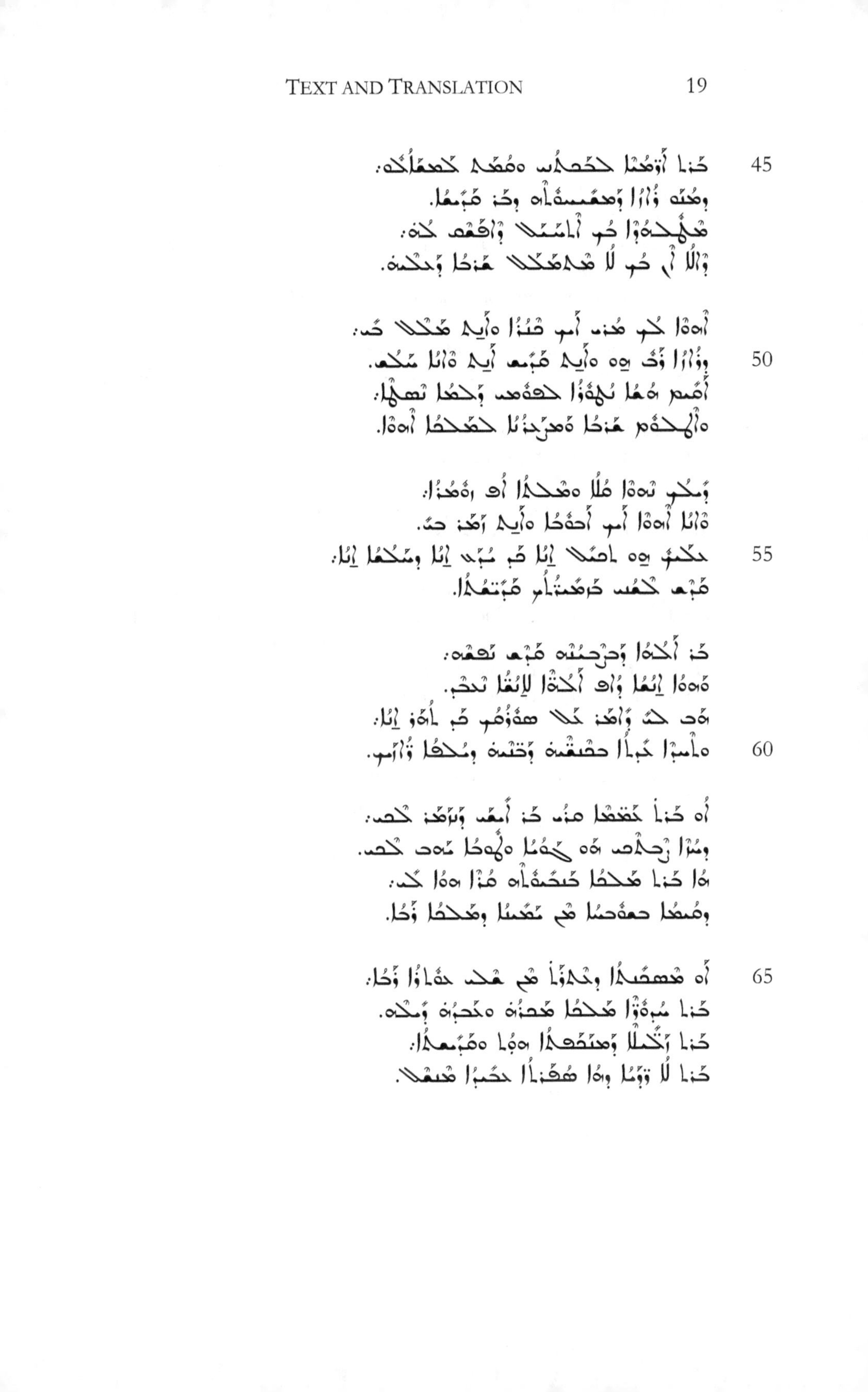

	Daughter of the ignorant who has vanquished the sages in disputation.
70	Daughter of the uncircumcised who put the circumcised too in wonder.
	O Daughter of the impure, why do you investigate concerning the Holy One?
	Here you are, pressing on in asking about the hidden mysteries!

'All your beauty has been hidden', said David,[11]
And behold, you have been adorned manifestly with vestments of excellent gold.
75 Behold, in your virginity, you have offered gifts to the King,
And virgins run after you, in holy fashion:[12]

With pleasure and joy of heart, they come to you,
For you have left the house of your parents and its defilement.[13]
See how baptism gives birth to new children for you,
80 So that you may send them to the entire world, having authority.
And the coming generations will remember you with your humility,
And the peoples of the earth will confess the Son in your courts.
'Listen my daughter, look and incline your ear', cries out David,[14]
And forget your people and do not remember the house of your father,

85 For, behold the king desires your beauty, O Daughter of light!
Worship him now, for He is your Lord, and also of your companions.[15]
Behold the rich assemble before you with their offerings,[16]
To seek your face, for the Son of the Holy One is in your chamber!

---

[11] Cfr. Ps. 45:13.
[12] Ps. 45:15–16.
[13] Cfr. Ps. 45:11.
[14] Ps. 45:11.
[15] Ps. 45:10–11.
[16] Ps. 45:13.

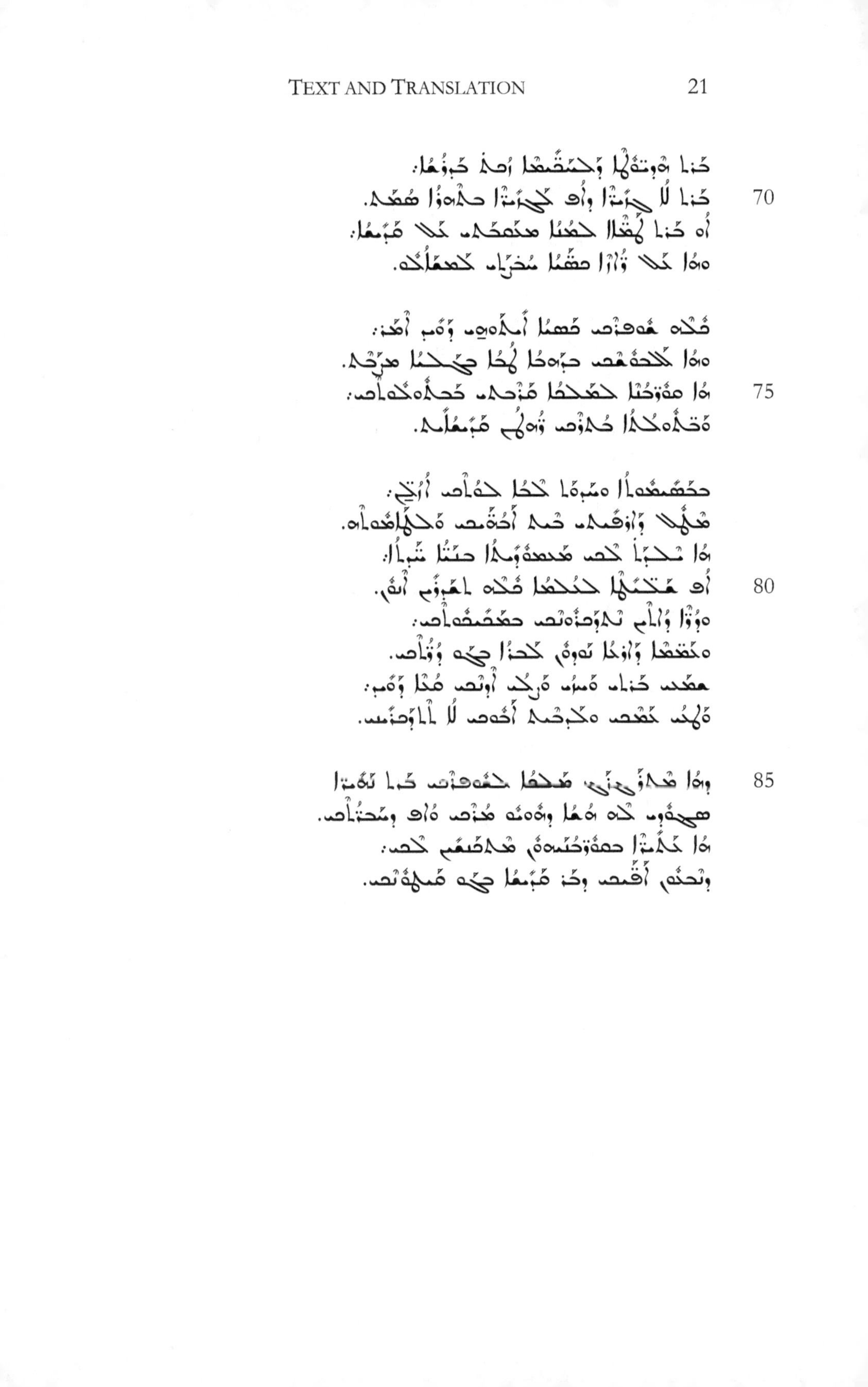

Behold, you have recognized Him from the swaddling clothes,
who He is, and whose Son.
90 And you saw the gifts that are piled before him by the mighty:
Incense for his glory, gold and for His might and lordship,[17]
Pure myrrh, symbol of his death and resurrection.

Look how, at the river, three witnesses became His proclaimers,[18]
The Father with His voice, and the (Holy) Sprit by appearing, and
    the Son through touch.
95 See how, by His fasting, He has conquered Satan for You,[19]
And by His wisdom, He has driven away and put to flight His
    temptations.

See how he had shown you (an example) when he healed the
    wounded,
Along with all the signs and wonders He performed in Judea.
Look how, on the mountain, among the new and old orders,
100 He made Himself shining and showed Himself to you that He is Son
    of the Holy One.

Look how, on a colt, you acclaimed Him, together with your children,[20]
And through the mouth of your children, you glorified Him with
    cries of Hosanna.
Look how, in the house of Simon, He allowed Himself to be per-
    fumed by the harlot.[21]
And He taught that you have authority to forgive debts.

105 He came, not to sanctify the righteous, who do not need it,[22]
But to call, absolve and to sanctify the impure of the earth.

---

[17] Mt. 2:11.
[18] Mt. 3:16–17.
[19] Mt. 4:2.
[20] Mt. 21:7; 15.
[21] Lk. 7: 36–37; cfr. Mt. 26:6–13; Mk. 14:3–9.
[22] Mt. 9:7.

90

95

100

105

Behold, His humiliation, mocking, insult and abuse,
And the crucifixion and sufferings that He endured, He has revealed and shown to you.

Look how, in the Upper-room, He gave his body and blood for your delight,[23]
110 To show that he came voluntarily to death.
Look how, He descended to the place of the dead and was placed (in the tomb) like (any other) dead person,
To show you that He has authority over the dead to raise (them).

Look how, by His resurrection, He consoled and gathered you, for you were scattered,
And for those in shame, He covered them in shame and justified[24] them.
115 Look how, in the Upper Room, when it was closed, He showed Himself to you,[25]
To show you that He can pass through solid objects.

See how, He showed you also (the place of) the spear and the nails,[26]
To drive away from you the phantasy of the Phantasiasts.
Look how, He assembled you on the Mount Olives, to see Him when he ascended,[27]
120 Lest you should doubt the promise that He had given you.

Look how, He sent for you, the tongues of fire and the Spirit,[28]
So that you should know that He has the same honour with his Father.
Behold, the Holy One dwells in sanctuary and sanctifies you,
And every day, you are spiritually enriched by him.

---

[23] Mk. 14:15ff.
[24] Or *scattered*, if we read *zrq* for *zdk*.
[25] Jn. 20:19–23; 26.
[26] Jn. 20:25; 27.
[27] Acts. 1:9–12
[28] Acts. 2:3.

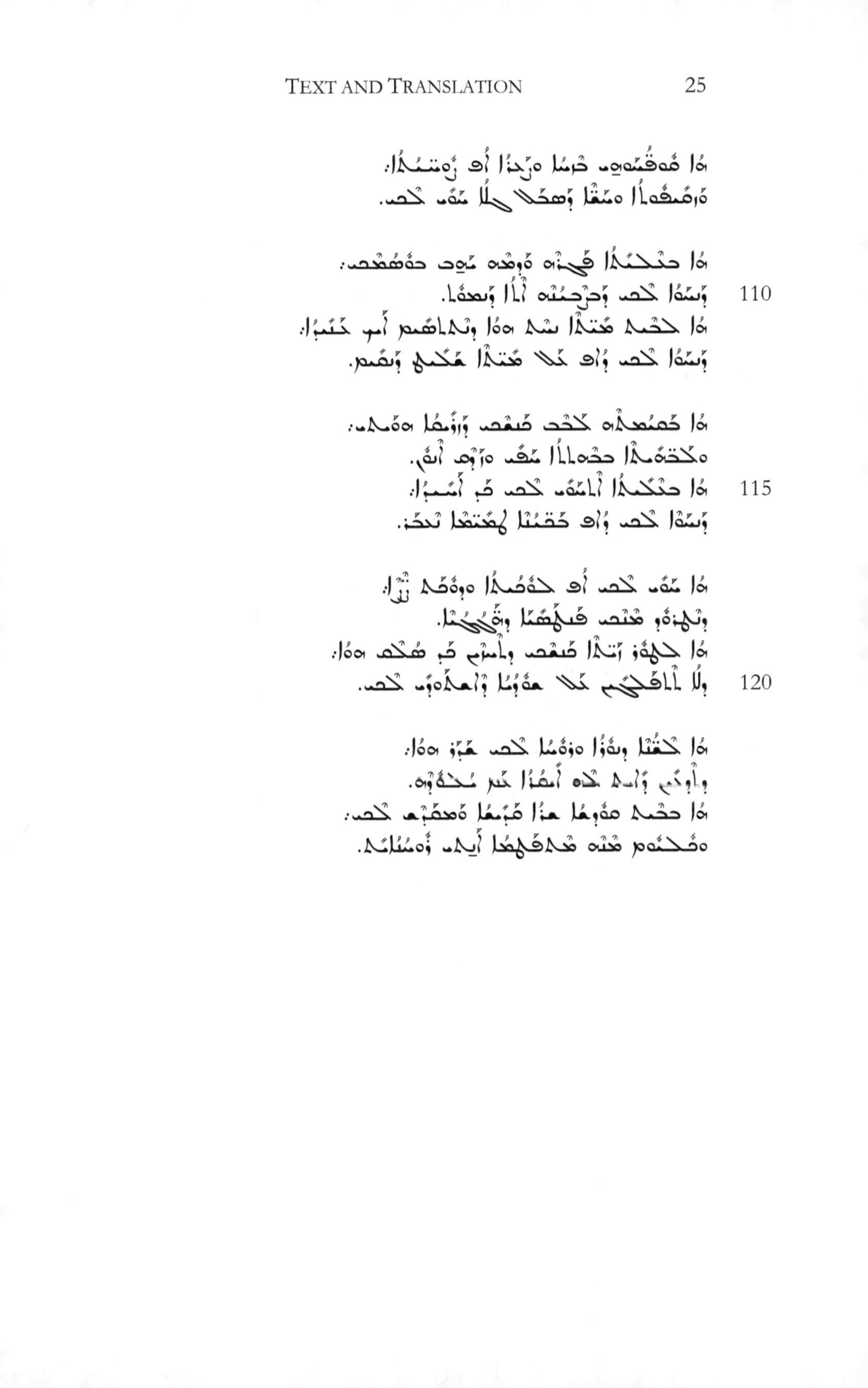

125 He has fed you with His body and given you His blood to drink,
   (and) His cross your strength,
His side has been pierced, so as to bear the fruit of baptism.[29]
The keys of the heights and the depths, He has given you, for He
   loves you,[30]
And He promised you through his words (that) He binds and looses.

He made your sanctuary a throne for Himself, and He dwells with you,[31]
130 And every day you converse with the King and He cherishes you.

In His mysteries, you rejoice and you take pride in Him and He
   rejoices in you,
And you are assured of all that He has done for you.

You do not doubt the kingdom and the height,
And you are assured of his divinity and also of His humanity.
135 A True One from the True One, without division,
And equal in power and in Kingdom and in creative ability.

For, while remaining God, in His love He became man,
And He was the same in power, might and heroism.
He was God even when he suffered the human limitations,
140 Also (He was) man, when He performed the divine actions.

O glorious one, who have learnt these hidden mysteries,
What mystery has hidden itself from your understanding?
I am amazed how your faith is,
So how shall I, so insignificant, dare to tell of you?

145 By the wonderful power of your faith, I approach,
O Christ, who became a voice in Paul, Speak in me!
Make me worthy to speak of You, O Son of the Holy One,
The Son of God who became Christ with humanity.

---

[29] Jn. 19:34.
[30] Mt. 16:19.
[31] Cfr. Heb. 9:24.

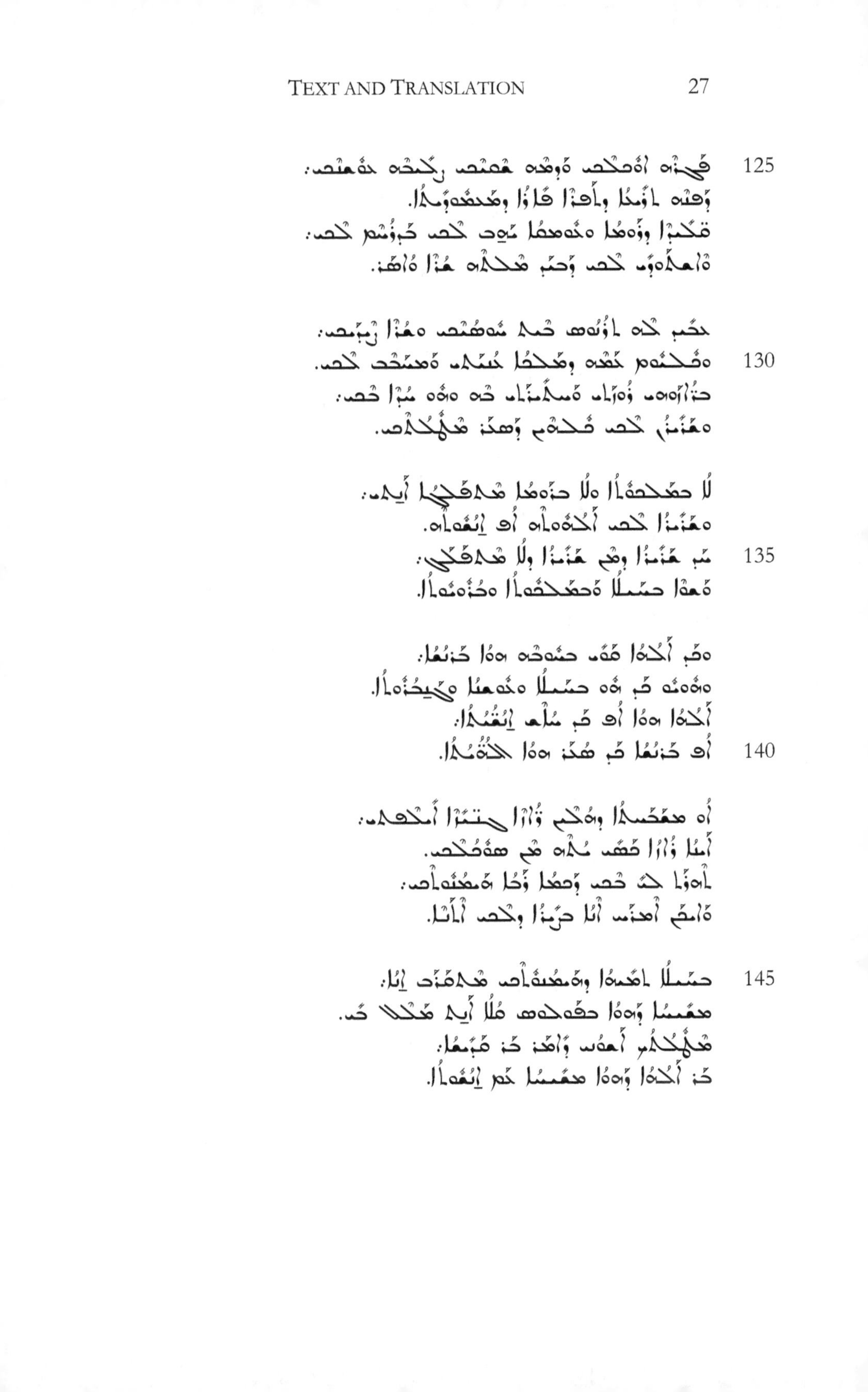

Reveal to Your Church, the great mystery of your anointing!
150 O Son of God, You have given us life by Your humility.
The day of Your self-abasement bears a mystery for the Daughter of luminaries,
And she desires to see clearly its interpretation.

O Bride of the Bridegroom, incline your ear with faith,
For these mysteries are understood only by faith.
155 And without it, the mystery cannot be listened to.
Whoever is wavering or doubting will not abide in you.

Let all the inquisitive and disputatious depart from you,
And those who are in doubt and investigate the truth.
Hold on to the simple, so that your faith remains simple.
160 Let the simple enter, and the cleverness keep its distance.

Let the lamb listen, for the investigation is reserved for the goats,
Seeing that the mysteries that are in you are too lofty for the tongue.
Let the sheep that recognize the voice of the shepherd rejoice at his sheepfold,[32]
Let the wolves depart, for they tear to pieces the mysteries with their inquiry.

165 Let the dove remain, and listen to the homily with faith,
Let the bird of prey that cunningly snatches (the fledglings) with words depart.
Let the dove, whose heart is filled with innocence, settle down;
Let the hawk that threatens to destroy every fledgling, be driven away.

Let the enemies depart and let the friends and the sons of the mysteries enter,
170 Let him who divides the Son of God not remain in you.[33]
The mystery is great and the wavering heart does not grasp it,
Nor can a broken vessel hold good oil.

---

[32] Jn. 10:16.

[33] The author refers to those who hold the doctrine of two hypostases as well as two natures.

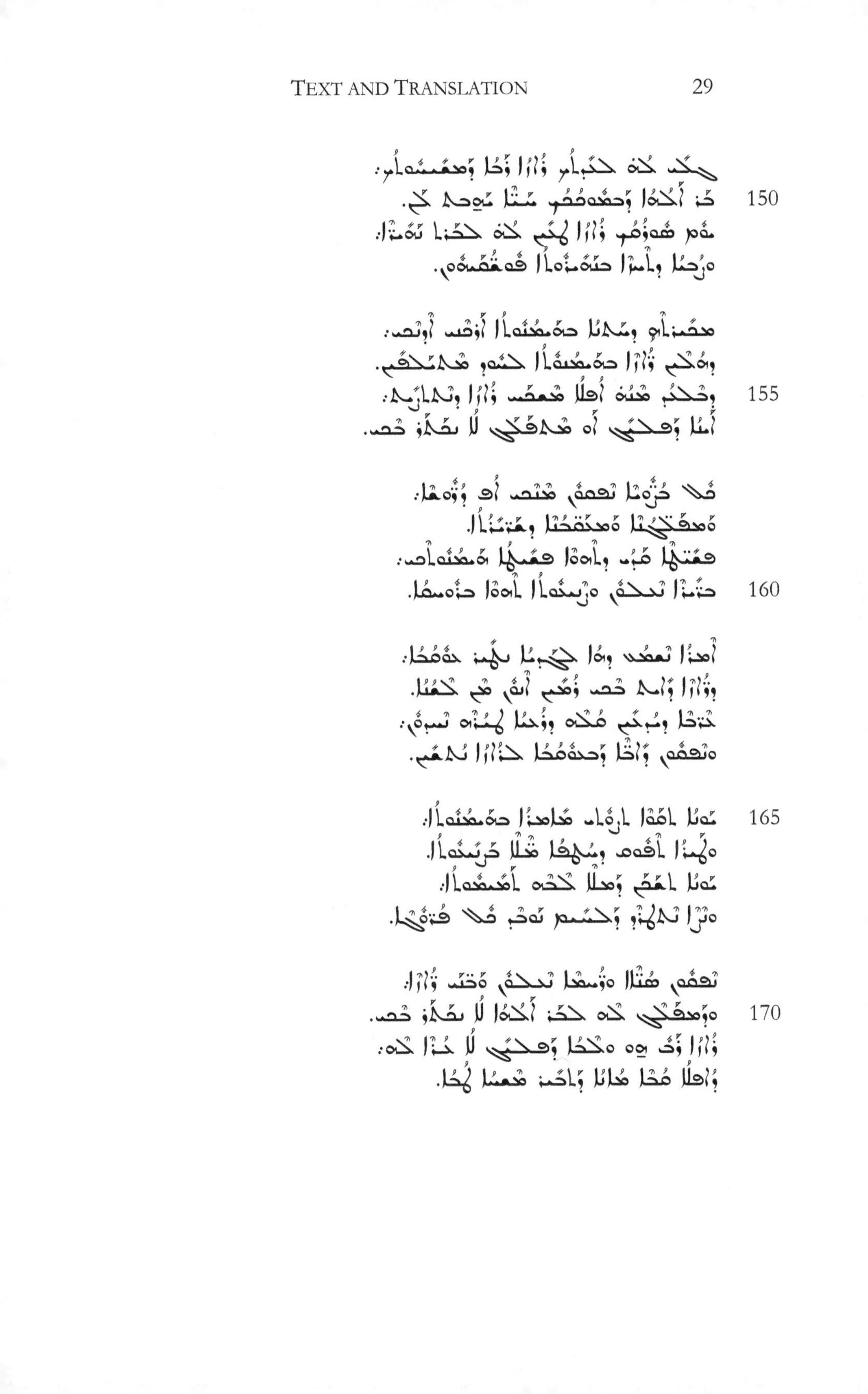

Faith consumes the Son of God (in) the bread,
And she drinks the wine, the type of His blood, and is true for Him.
175 Through the priest, she enters the sanctuary and she does not doubt,
For everything that she asks, she receives from him abundantly.

She bears the cross and in it she sees the Son of God,
She descends into the water and she does not doubt that it is Him that she puts on.
Similarly, here also she wants to believe firmly without investigation,
180 Truly with the oil of holiness, she puts on the Son of God.

He is the Lord, the bread, the drink, as well as the absolution,
And He is the crucified One, and He is always present and waits for us.
It is He who weaves vestments always to clothe us.
And it is He who became the oil of holiness that gladdens us.

185 In the beginning, Adam was created as a new creature,
But because he became old, He came again and renewed him.
In the beginning, the Father fashioned Adam from the earth,[34]
And now, He assumed him and made him new with His own passions.

Him who had become old and sold himself to pleasures,
190 He made him free, and he became new by the passion of his Son.

Because he had ruined his five senses with vanities,
On the fifth day [Thursday], he destroyed them in a fivefold way.[35]

And therefore Moses wrote five books,
So that through five, he might perfect the five (senses) which had vanquished (Adam);
195 After five generations, Israel went up from Egypt,
Seeing that they had immersed their five senses in pleasures.

---

[34] Gen. 2:7.
[35] Cfr. Bar Kepha, *Myron*, ch.26.

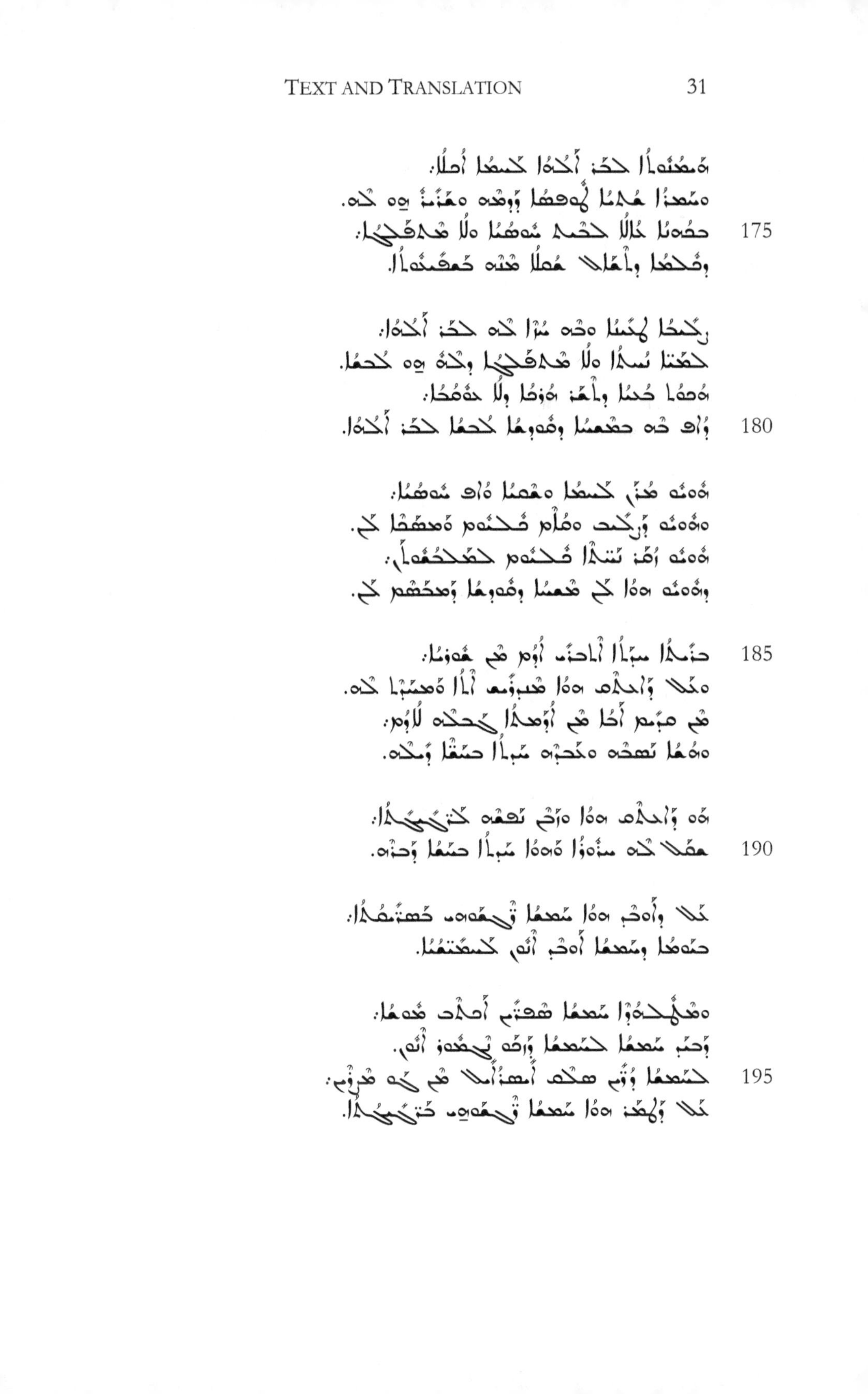

Five talents, a symbol of the perfecting of the five senses,
Did our Lord give to the good servant to trade with.[36]
He purified and cleansed the senses of the soul and the senses of the body,
200 And gladly, he entered into the joy of his master and became heir.[37]

And through the virgins, our Lord depicted the bridal chamber of light,[38]
He found the five, with their lamps alight.
Therefore the Holy Church celebrates a feast today,[39]
So that all the mysteries may be wisely gathered to her.

205 And the light of the day perfects this mystery,
For the night filed with error has been passed away and the light reigns.
And therefore, this mystery cries out to those who are discerning,
That, it will always proceed clothed with victory under the guise of light.

Let nobody fear to call upon the Lord in time day,
210 For the daylight (consists) in the works that please Him.[40]
By the light of the Lord, he who wishes will see the light,[41]
He who keeps his word recognizes Him, who is light.

For during the daylight it is written that the Lord commanded His friends
Concerning him who possesses works of light, and not those of darkness.

---

[36] Mt. 25:16; 21.
[37] Mt. 25:21.
[38] Mt. 25:10.
[39] Consecration of Myron on Maundy Thursday, George, *Com.*, p. 20.
[40] Cfr. Jn. 11:9.
[41] Cfr. Ps. 36:10.

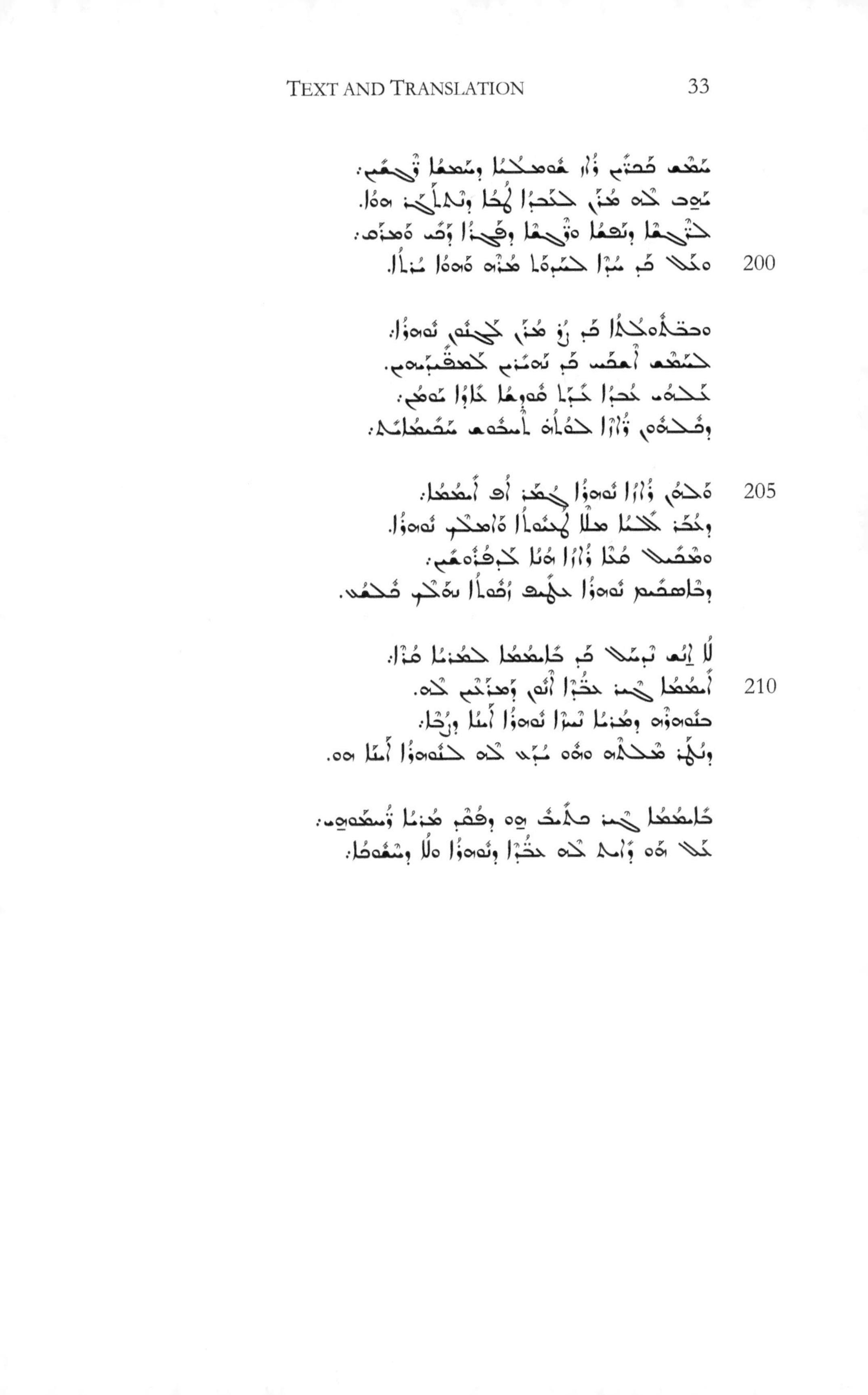

215   Therefore at the third hour of the day,[42]
     This oil which is full of life is consecrated.
     In the case of the Lord of the vineyard, who hired workers for his vineyard,[43]
     It was at the third hour that the unemployed entered the vineyard for the first time.[44]
     I suppose that it was at the third hour that Adam ate (the fruit) of the tree,
220   At the sixth hour, He ascended on the cross for him.

     And I that was at the third hour, He was suspended, repaying the debt of Adam,
     At the ninth (hour) He returned him to Paradise, in the person of the robber.[45]
     The bond that the serpent wrote at the third hour,
     Christ tore it up at the third hour on Golgotha.

225   Therefore let the Church walk on the path of the Bridegroom,
     And let her reveal to her children all the mysteries that are in the Scriptures.
     Let the world learn that they were symbolized for her from the beginning:
     The fathers and the righteous, the just and the saints,

     [All] the ancients have depicted for her the type of the anointing,
230   With parables the just of old took delight in it,
     Veiled and hidden, it was set out and placed in the prophecy:
     [The oil] anoints kings and perfects priests, according to the Law.

---

[42] In the Syrian Orthodox tradition, Myron is always consecrated during the celebration of the Eucharist, that in the forenoon. The celebration begins at third hour. Cfr. VARGHESE, *Les Onctions*, pp. 268–272; 310–327; Bar Hebraeus, *Nomocanon*, III-3, pp. 50–53.

[43] Mt. 20:3.

[44] Mt. 20:3–4.

[45] Lk. 23:43–44.

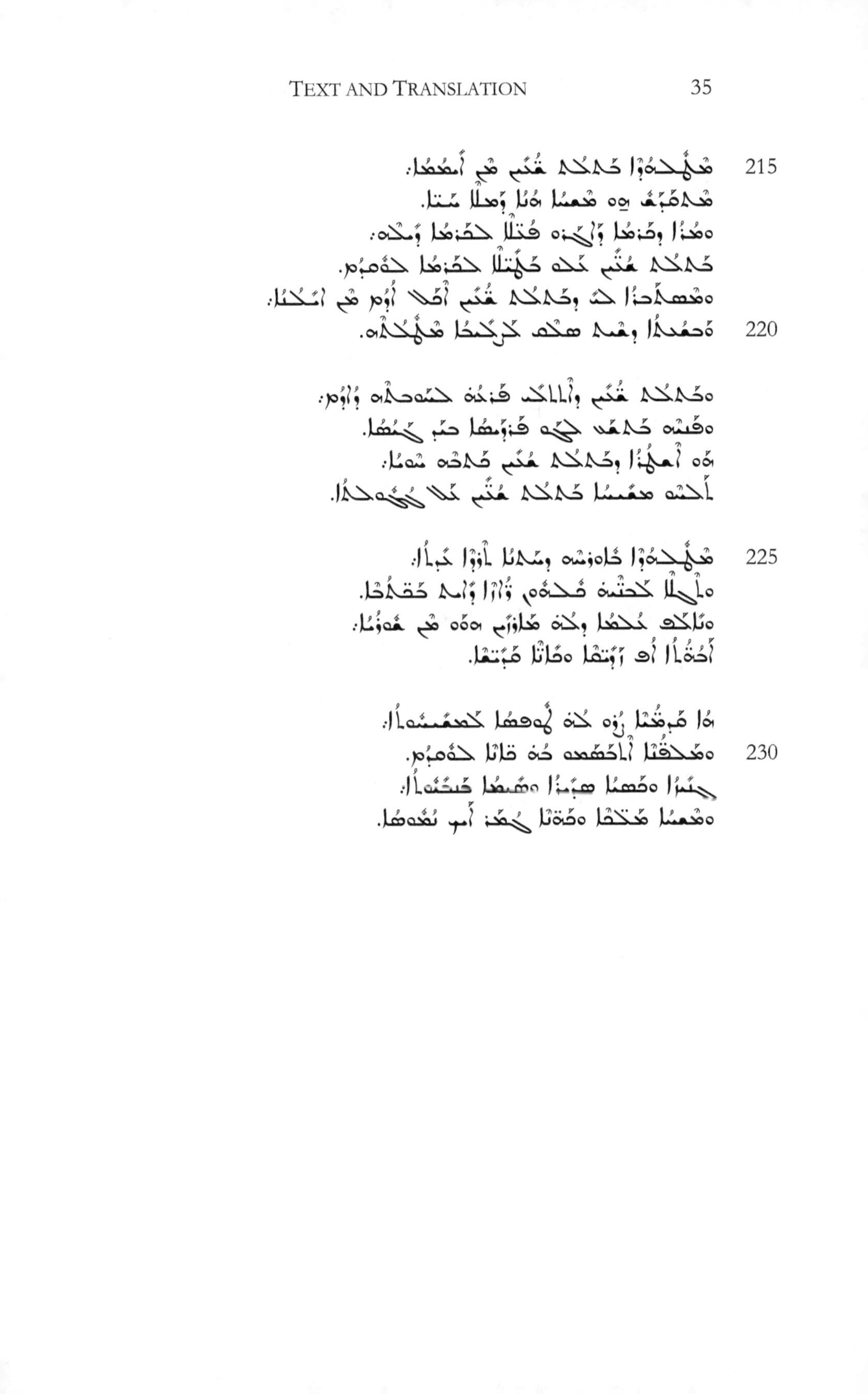

It sent good tidings to Noah the just inside the ark,[46]
Indicating to him, 'It is through the oil that your salvation has been granted'.
235 The mystery of the anointing seethed in the olive branch,
And it plucked a leaf and gave it to the dove to convey to the just man.[47]

Christ and the oil were represented there mysteriously,
(And also) the Spirit of love, the good tidings of mercy and salvation.
With the oil Jacob prefigured the Church, when he fled[48];
240 Manifesting the symbols of the anointing in symbolic fashion,

For it is a house of refuge for a person who flees, (and) he will be protected with it.
Spiritual people are not perfected, except by the oil.
In his prophecy, Moses prefigured this oil,[49]
And about its composition, he learned thus from the Holy One:
245 With skill, he should bring choice sweet spices,
And pressed oil of fine olive and he should compound (them together).
And from this oil and the choice sweet spices which he had brought,[50]
The Levite made (the oil) of anointing, as he was commanded.

And with it, he anointed Aaron, that venerable high priest,[51]
250 And with it, he sanctified all his sons and sealed them,
And anointed the basin, which was the type of baptism,[52]
And the table upon which the high priest offers sacrifice,[53]

---

[46] Gen. 8:11.
[47] Gen. 8:11.
[48] Gen. 28:18.
[49] Ex. 30:22–23.
[50] Ex. 30:22–31.
[51] Ex. 40:13.
[52] Ex. 40:11.
[53] Ex. 40:11.

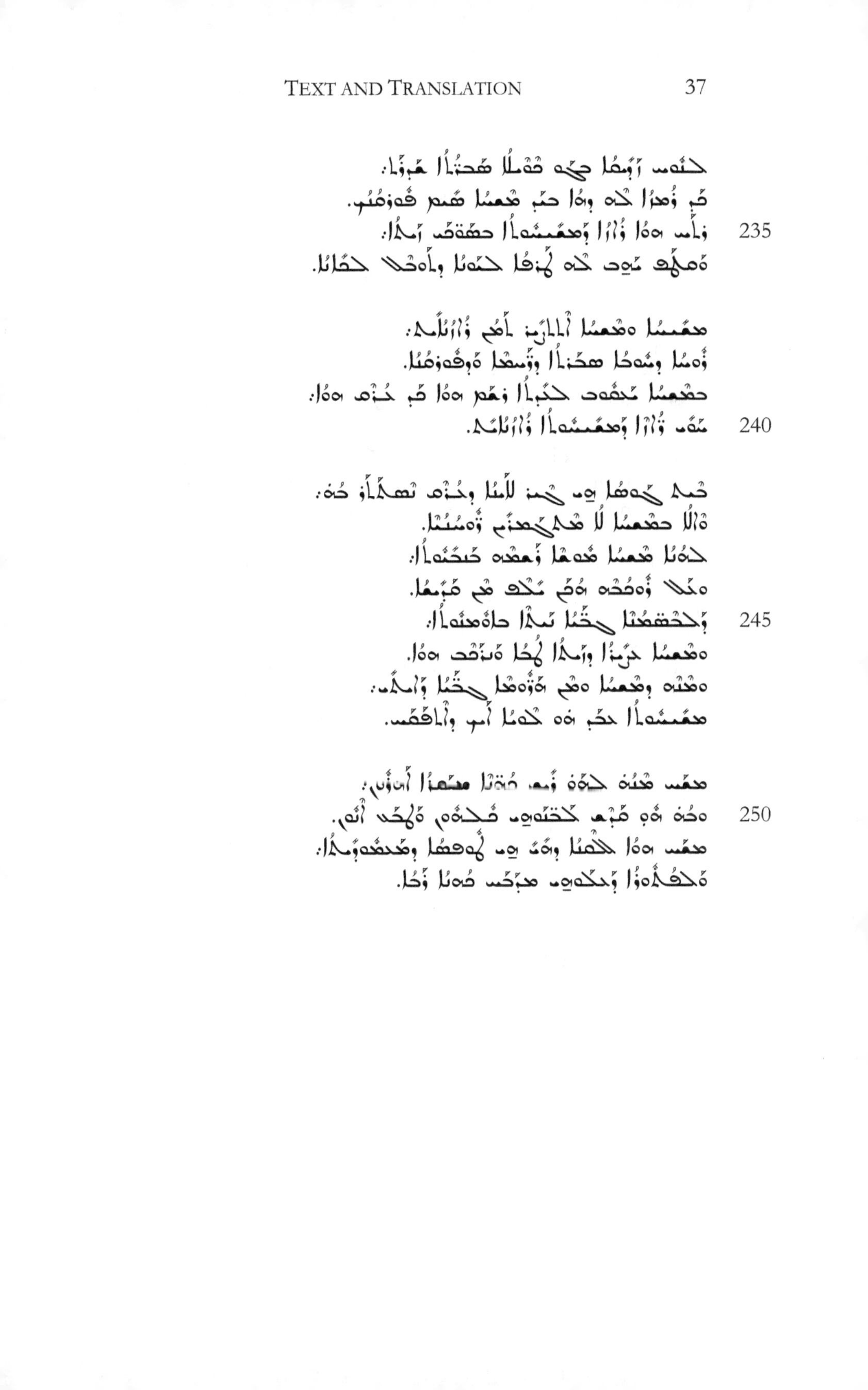

So that they might represent the anointing of the Son of God,
Who is also the priest, and the Lord of priests, as well as the High Priest.
255 Everyone who transgresses against the compounding of this (oil)
Will die an evil death, for he has brought destruction upon himself.[54]

Therefore you alone, the humble (Moses) are to prepare it,
And for your generations, it shall be for my memory, as I desire.
O Hebrew, who is radiantly clothed in the image of the Father,
260 Who hastens to depict the new symbol of the image of the Son,

Namely, the anointing of the Son of God with the humanity
Depicting (it) in the oil and the sweet spices and in the composition.
He did not reveal the mystery of his embodiment, except to His Father,
For He alone knows how He mingled Himself with us.

265 The matter concerning Him is hidden and even from all the angels above.
And the Father alone anointed Him in the flesh and sent Him to us.[55]
He, by His will, He emptied Himself and became man,[56]
And it is the Holy Spirit who accomplished the operation.

For they are one, and of one will, hidden among them,
270 And He granted this mystery to the priest so that He might be adorned with it.
The mystery that is hidden to those who above, He revealed to those below,
So that the world might see that the earthly beings have become spirituals beings.
While the Levite was delighted in the great mystery,
And looking for, the time when he would see it clearly.

---

[54] Ex. 30:33.
[55] Cfr. Acts. 10:38; Hb. 1:9.
[56] Cfr. Phil. 2:7.

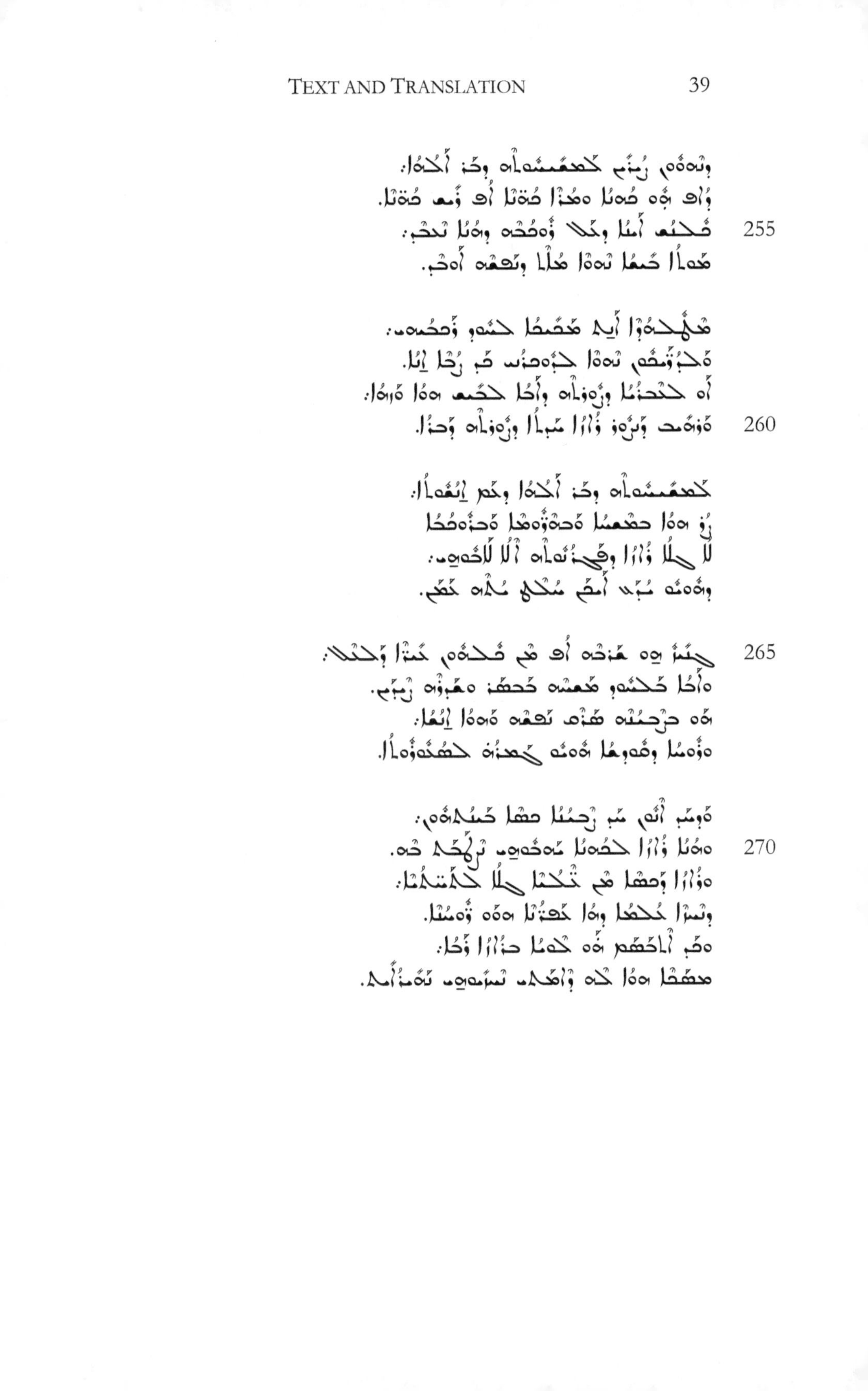

| 275 | He kept (the oil) carefully in a horn with expectation,[57]
For it was held in honour for the memory of the coming generations.

And when a king, prophet or a priest arose among the people,
They would be anointed with the holy oil, according to the Law.
And for this reason, the elect Samuel was commanded[58]
| 280 | By God to anoint the Son of Jesse as king,

When the shepherd boy, insignificant and despised, was coming,
The horn became eager to anoint his pure body.[59]
David bore the mysteries of the Son that were hidden in him,
Similarly, the river at His meeting surged, when He descended.

| 285 | In the midst of his brothers David received the anointing,
Similarly, Our Lord (received) it for the crucifixion in the centre of the universe.
For this reason (David) sees him as though this had (already) happened,
relating the mystery of the anointing of the Son of God:

Behold God, your God, more than your companions,[60]
| 290 | Has anointed you wonderfully with the oil of life and gladness.[61]
For you have hated wickedness and loved justice,
And mercy is infused upon your holy lips.

Your sceptre will last forever in righteousness,
And your throne will be exalted above those of the kings and the rulers.[62]
| 295 | And with pure Myron and sweet spices have your garments been perfumed,
And in the assemblies there breathes the fragrance of your sweet spices.

---

[57] That is the horn of the oil.
[58] 1 Sam. 16:12.
[59] 1 Sam. 16:13.
[60] Ps. 45:8.
[61] Ps. 45:7.
[62] Ps. 45:6.

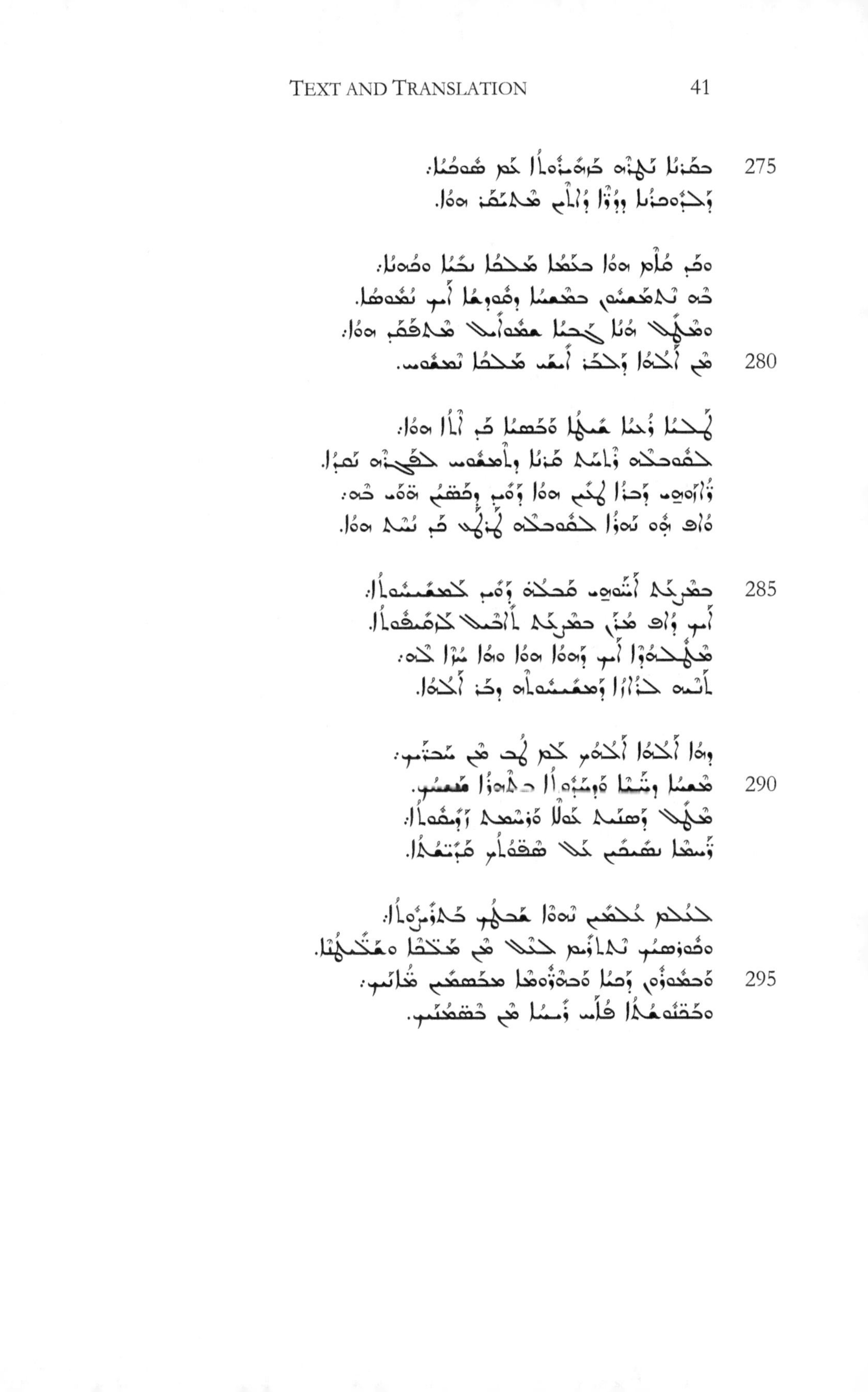

The mystery of the anointing was near to Solomon also,
For he received abundantly the wisdom of the Lord, even when he was a child.[63]
And with the oil, He signed the son of Yamshi to make him king.[64]
300 Similarly the Church anoints kings spiritually,

Namely, everyone who receives the mark of the Lord in baptism
There by having authority to rule in truth over all the passions.
With the oil, kings received a mighty crown and they ruled,
And with the oil, the priests received priesthood.

305 Again the prophets were anointed with it and they prophesied,
The mystery is wonderful, hidden and veiled, and cannot be examined.
And when the time has come to reveal itself to the nations,
The Church ran with the assembly of her children, and she received it.

And when He appeared on earth, He received it from the tongue-tied Moses,[65]
310 Receiving the priesthood from John,[66]
He gathered in prophecy, as well as the priesthood.
For He is the Lord, Priest and the King and the Lord of the prophets.

And when He ascended, He extended His right hand over His disciples,
And made them priests, so that they might give (it) to the entire world.
315 So as to instruct and to convert the nations of the earth,
The Saviour of the whole creation sent them out;

---

[63] 1 Kgs 3:12.

[64] 2 Kgs. 9:2 (*Peshitta*).

[65] Ex. 4:10.

[66] The Syriac fathers usually speak of the continuity of the priesthoods in the Old and New Testaments. The expression, 'Christ received priesthood from John' simply means this continuity.

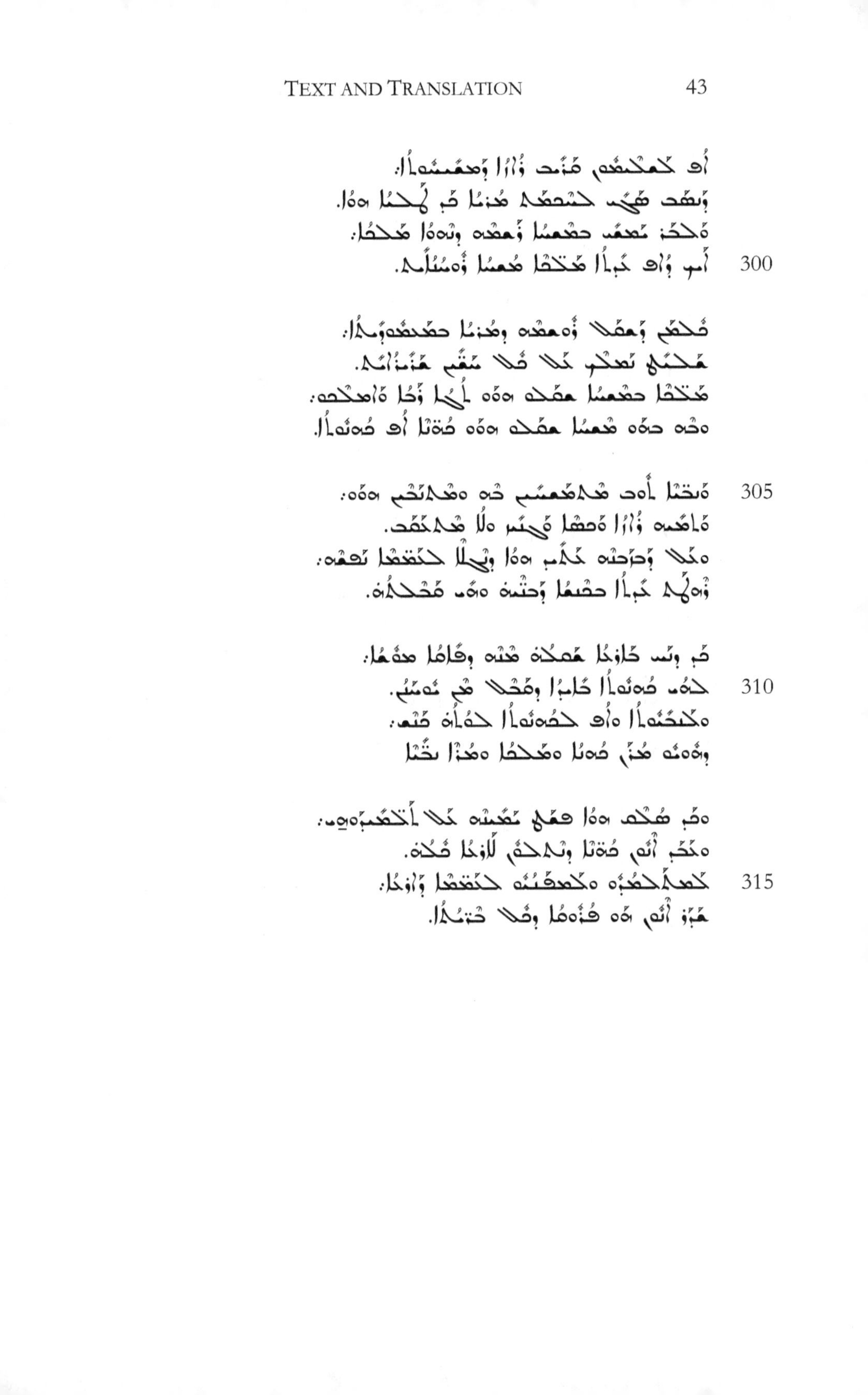

With the Holy Spirit, He strengthened them and taught them,
So that they might minister the mysteries depicted by the ancients.
The bishop is wrapped in the likeness of light,[67] and with fear,
320 He enters alone inside the Holy of Holies.

And as the Father, in His glorious light, is hidden from the angels,
The high priest also is hidden in the sanctuary.
And on behalf of himself, he puts incense for the absolution,
And then he approaches the great mystery with fear.

325 There are two (kinds of) oils in his hands to combine,[68]
So as to signify there the divinity and the humanity.

He makes it one, so that (the oil) shall become pleasant in its fragrance,
For Christ is One, and His divinity is incomprehensible.

O man, the mystery that you minister is amazing!
330 See that you do not forget that you are man, not God!
Do not exalt yourself because you have taken the role of the hidden Father:
The reminder of the world is placed on your vestments with letters.

Lest your spirit become proud of (the place) where you have reached,
Let the earth be placed before you, O son of dust!
335 Lest you become haughty and forget your nature, when you see your glory,
You have been appointed by grace, it is not by your nature that you have it.

---

[67] Until the 12th century, the bishops used to wear white vestments (*paino*) for the consecration of the Myron. Cfr. Jacob of Edessa, *Myron*, # 19; Bar Kepha, *Myron*, ch.29.

[68] The mixing of the two oils is not mentioned in the prose commentary attributed to George. *Com.*, p. 21.

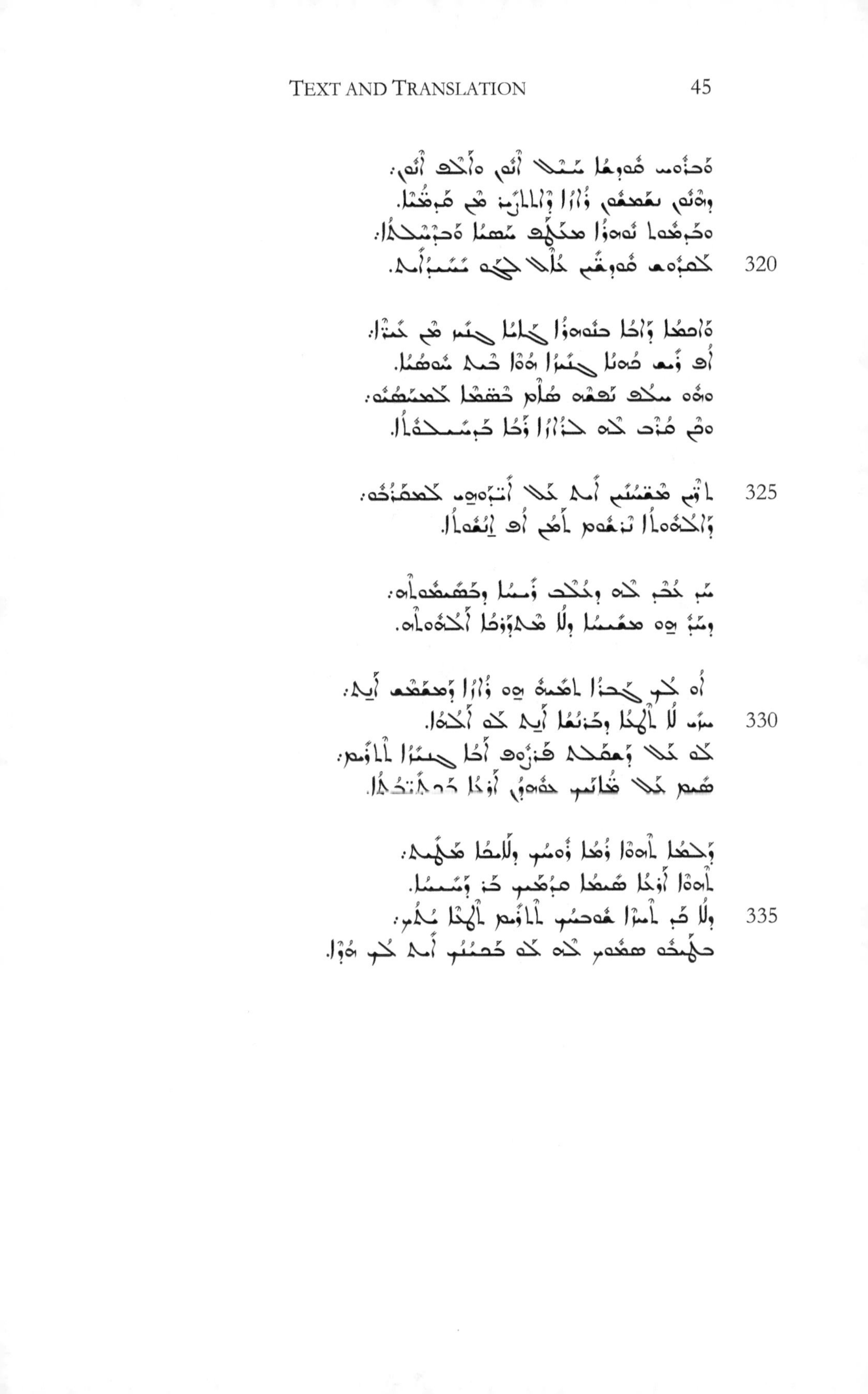

Let your glory be mixed with fear, lest you slip and fall.
Let the humility of the great Moses be with you.
Satan is used to dare to enter the Holy of Holies,
340 Invoke the Lord, so that He rebukes, destroys and gets rid of him.

Behold, you have been made god on earth and also the one who perfects,
Because you have received anointing that signs the children of God.
Put on the humility of the Son of God and think of Him!
Imitate Him, who girded a towel like a servant.[69]

345 Let the example of your Master and His abasement be manifested in you,
So that, being a god, in the mystery, you may make (others) also gods.
Come out from the hidden inner rooms, let we see your mysteries,
For your flock is here, listening for your voice, (for) you have greatly delayed.

He proceeds forth and comes out like the sun clad with rays.
350 And he holds the flask of gold in which there is the new manna.[70]
It is not the oil from the rock that his hands hold,
But the pure Myron hidden in the bosom of His Father.

It is not the horn which anoints kings and the nations of the earth,
But (the oil) that perfects the children to the Father with holiness.
355 It is not of the plants that quickly lose their fragrance,
But a fruit, whose fragrance surpasses all the sweet spices.
He holds the flask and covers it with beautiful wings,
And he accomplishes it only with twelve sharers in the mysteries.[71]

---

[69] Jn. 13:5.

[70] Here the author refers to the procession with the bottle of the Myron. According to George's commentary, Myron is carried in a vessel of gold or silver or glass.

[71] The author refers to the twelve deacons carrying twelve fans; see also, George, *Com.*, p. 22. According to Jacob of Edessa, the procession with the Myron was accompanied by twelve fans, twelve censors and twelve lights, Jacob, *Myron*, # 15; 17; 18. In the later tradition, 12 priests

---

carry 12 censors, 12 deacons fans and 12 sub-deacons candles. See Bar Hebraeus, *Nomocanon*, III-1, Bedjan, pp. 31–34.

When our Lord walked on the earth, He hid Himself,
360   And the twelve tribes did not understand their prophets.

He was hidden in His Father just as (the Myron) is now in the hands of the bishop,
And the prophets speak of Him obscurely in mystery.
Twelve wings (symbolize) the twelve tribes, the sons of Jacob,
From whom the prophets came out and prophesied about the Holy One.

365   For He has six-winged Seraphim in the heights,[72]
Who glorify Him in six-fold way with their hovering.
The fiery Cherubim, carry Him with great wonder,[73]
For through them He has shown the type that foreshadows the absolution.

Twelve censers go before him, for it is by the twelve,[74]
370   That the fragrance of the Gospel spread in the whole world.
Even if they will become twelve by twelve in duplication,
Son of Jesse symbolized it through his revelation.

Again lamps go in rows among the censers,
Symbolizing the doctors and commentators of the secrets.
375   For, with their teaching, they were like lights for the Church,
And she was illuminated with their divine wisdom.

With these choirs, the choirs go out with hymns,
And they escort the mystery that the bishop holds in his hands.
They stop at the north in the beginning, and this symbolizes
380   That they with withhold heroically the Accuser who blows (from the north).

---

[72] Is. 6:2.
[73] Ezek 10.
[74] Cfr. George, *Com.*, p. 22. However, in the commentary, it is not said that the number of the censors was twelve.

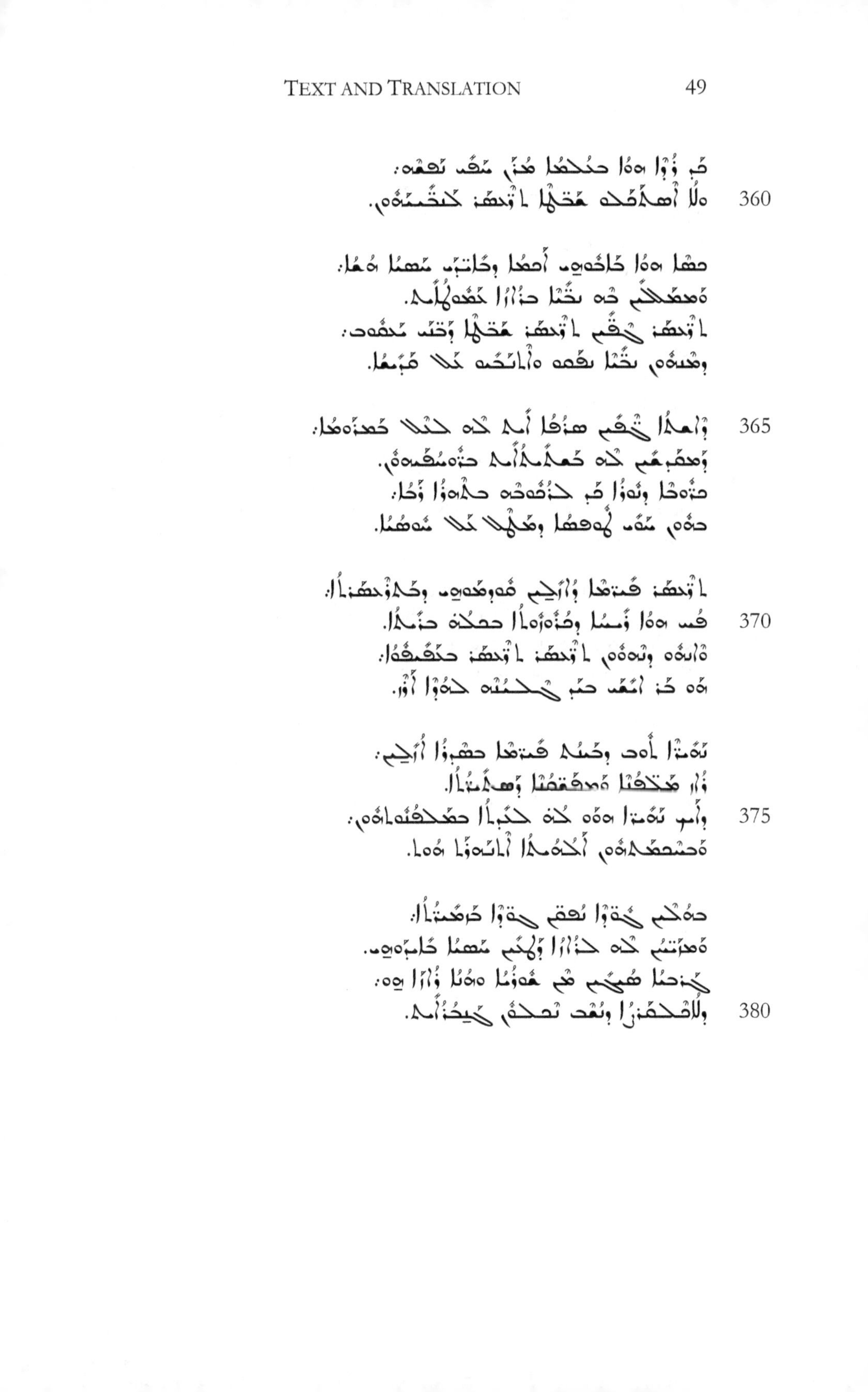

He proceeds solemnly like a bridegroom from the nuptial chamber,
And all that are assembled give voice with their haps.
Taking his harp in his hands, David exults,
He [now] dances better than [his] dance before the ark.[75]
385 You have raised my horns above those of the wild ox, O Son of God![76]
Also You have sprinkled me with the fragrant oil of holiness.[77]
You have been found by me, as You searched for me, O Good Shepherd,
With the holy oil, anoint my head, according to Your promise.[78]

May your hand help me against my enemies who surround me,
390 By you, may I be strengthened, and may I conquer them with courage.
The ranks are long and the choirs shout with holiness,
Facing the west, upon which You are mounted, O Lord our Lord![79]

Who taught us to flee from the morning star,[80]
Who makes his angels resemble light by his guile.[81]
395 For, he also, through pride let the great Sun of Justice,[82]
Set, apart from him, and he remained dark.

They come to the south that always bears light,[83]
To show us that He loves good works.
And whoever is illuminated, and his heart loves justice,
400 To him the Only-Begotten comes, with His Father,

---

[75] 2 Sam. 6:5.
[76] Ps. 92:10.
[77] Cfr. Ps. 89:21.
[78] Cfr. Ps. 23:5.
[79] Cfr. Ps. 68:5.
[80] Cf. Is. 14:12.
[81] Cf. 2 Cor. 11:14.
[82] Mal. 4:2.
[83] The procession reaches the southern side.

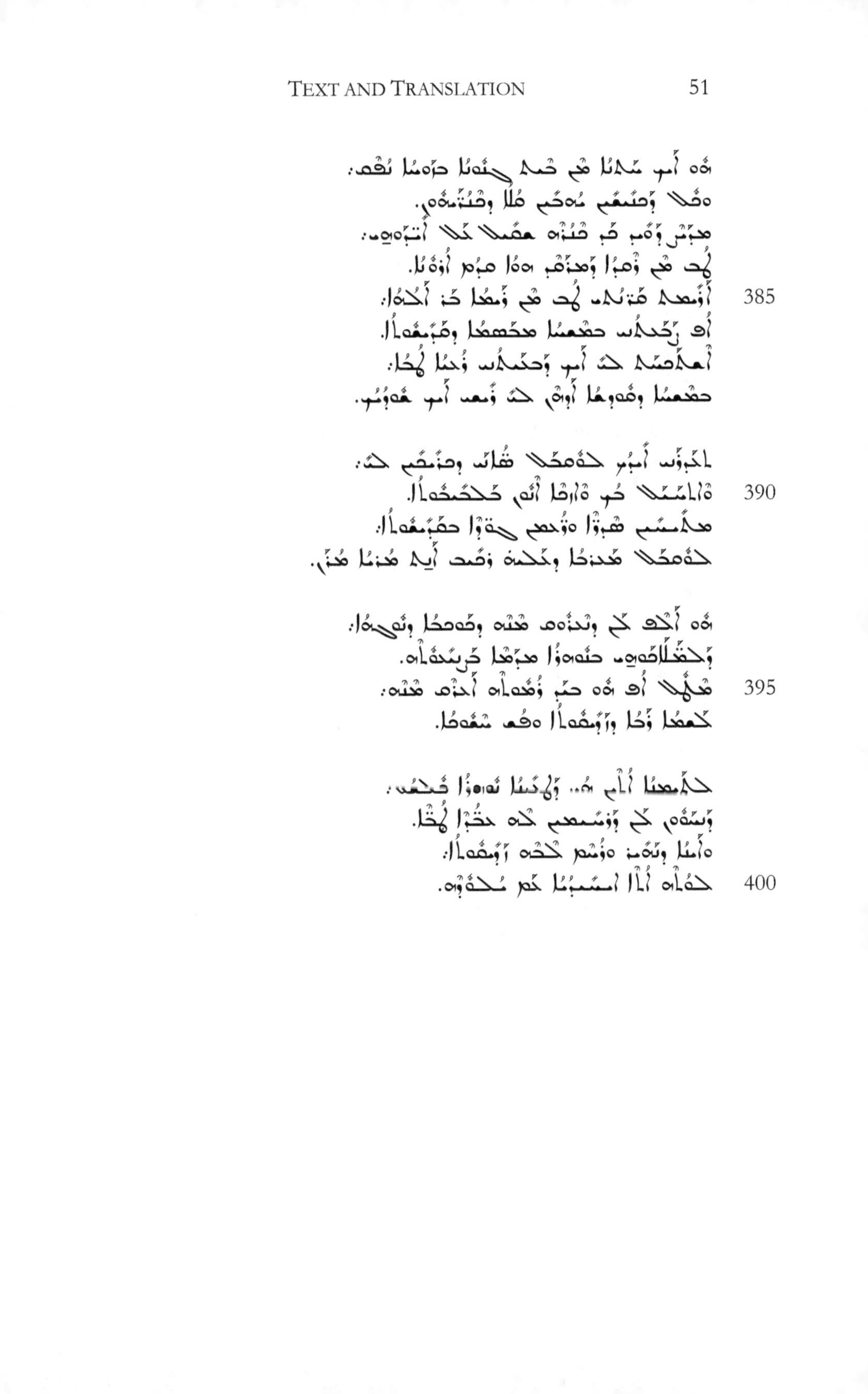

And He makes a dwelling place with him as he said,[84]
For Our Lord is Light, He dwells always in the enlightened.
The light of the sun courses the south and darks in the west.
But our Sun leaves the north and comes to the south.[85]

405　His flames brighten all parts luminously,
With awe, He enters the sanctuary majestically.
Lift up your heads, O doors with tranquility![86]
For the mighty King enters and He carries beatitude.
Holy city! Receive the Holy One with holiness,
410　For the mountain Pharan has sent Him to you, as it is written.[87]
Behold the Lord comes from the south, cries out the prophet,[88]
Rise and receive Him with your beautiful songs!

Extend tent-cords and expand your tents vigilantly,[89]
So that He who enriches the mind may enter and dwell in your palaces.
415　He places the flask on the altar symbolically,
As He was suspended on the wood of the crucifixion.[90]

On our behalf, He sanctified Himself by emptying Himself,
He who is eternally holy and divine with His Father.
With serene utterances, the bishop cries out to God,
420　And with songs full of mysteries, he intercedes.

---

[84] Jn. 14:23.

[85] The procession leaves the sanctuary from the northern side, and goes out by the northern door, moves in anti-clockwise direction and reaches the west and then the south. According to Syriac tradition, Christ came down from the height (north) of His divinity to the lower condition (south) of our humanity. Cfr. Bar Salibi, *Myron*, ch. 23.

[86] Ps. 24:7.

[87] Cfr Hab. 3:3.

[88] Dt. 33:2; Hab. 3:3.

[89] Cfr. Is. 54:2.

[90] As the procession returns to the sanctuary, the bishop places the bottle on the altar.

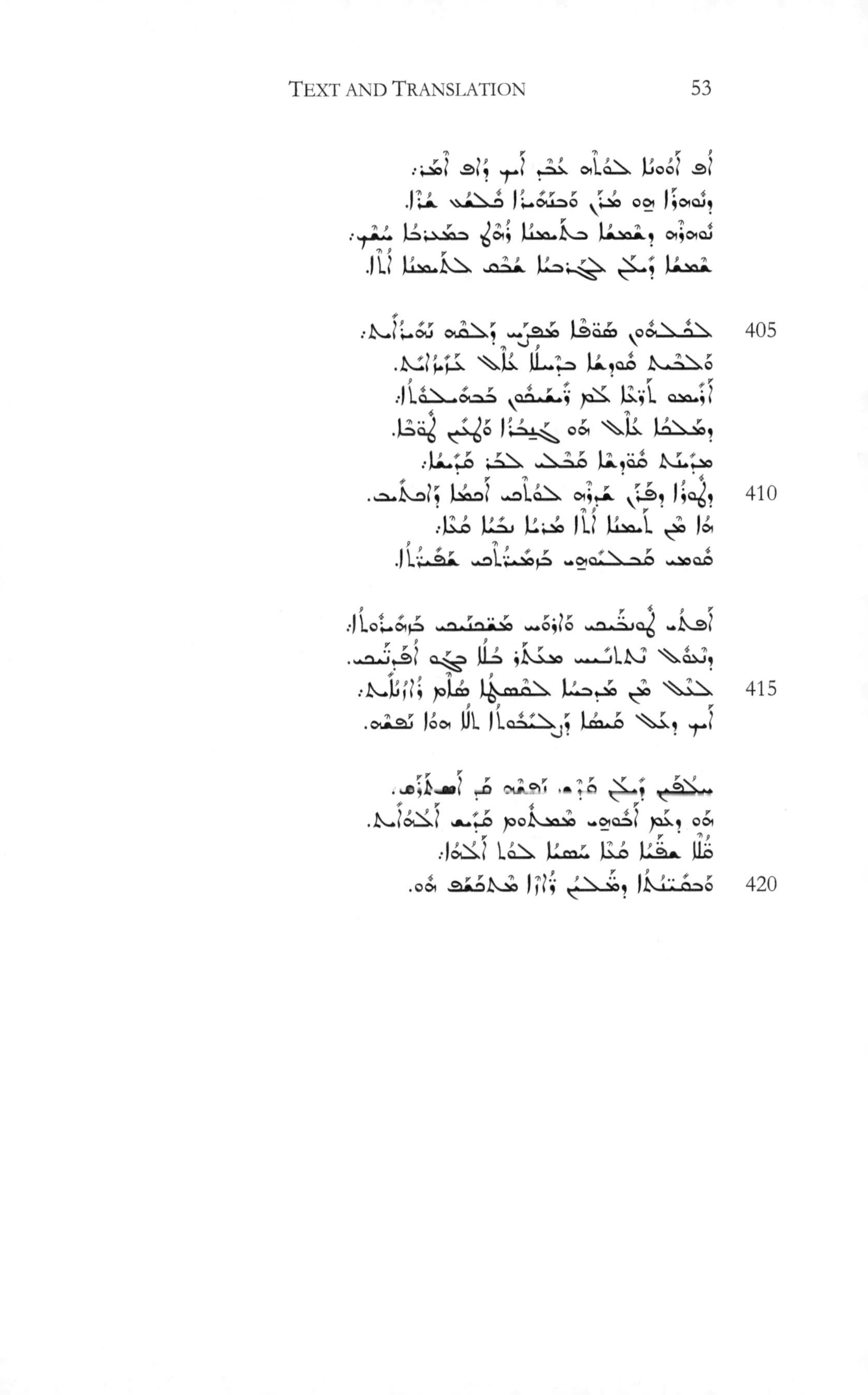

He ministers the mysteries, and with sighs, he asks for mercy,
And he stands upright and bows down and prostrates himself and groans
And he calls the Father, commemorating His Only-Begotten (Son)
And His voluntary abasement for us.

425 O Holy One, who is sanctified by the saints above,
Send Your Spirit who sanctifies all, so that He might perfect the mysteries.
That Holy One, who proceeds in holy fashion from You,
Who, through the prophets, apostles and the just

Spoke and taught truly all the mysteries,
430 Who is equal to You and to Your Only-Begotten in essence,
And who, with authority, confers holiness to every saint,
And who, as God, gives life according to His will.

And may He complete and perfect this oil with holiness,
So that all the mysteries of the Holy Church may be signed with it.
435 May it receive the power to seal the water of baptism,[91]
So that all the trees shall grow, may give fruits in your name.

May the senses of the soul be marked by it for protection,
And may the person filled with newness be strengthened by it;
May the altars be consecrated by it for the spiritual sacrifices;
440 And may the soul and the body be healed spiritually by it;

May the rational sheep be signed with it and may they receive life (by it);
May they be armed by it against the wolves that are thirsty for the prey.
May the power of the Evil One be overcome, who fights against us;
By His anointing, may the Lord destroy his crafty actions.

---

[91] Refers to the consecration of the baptismal water.

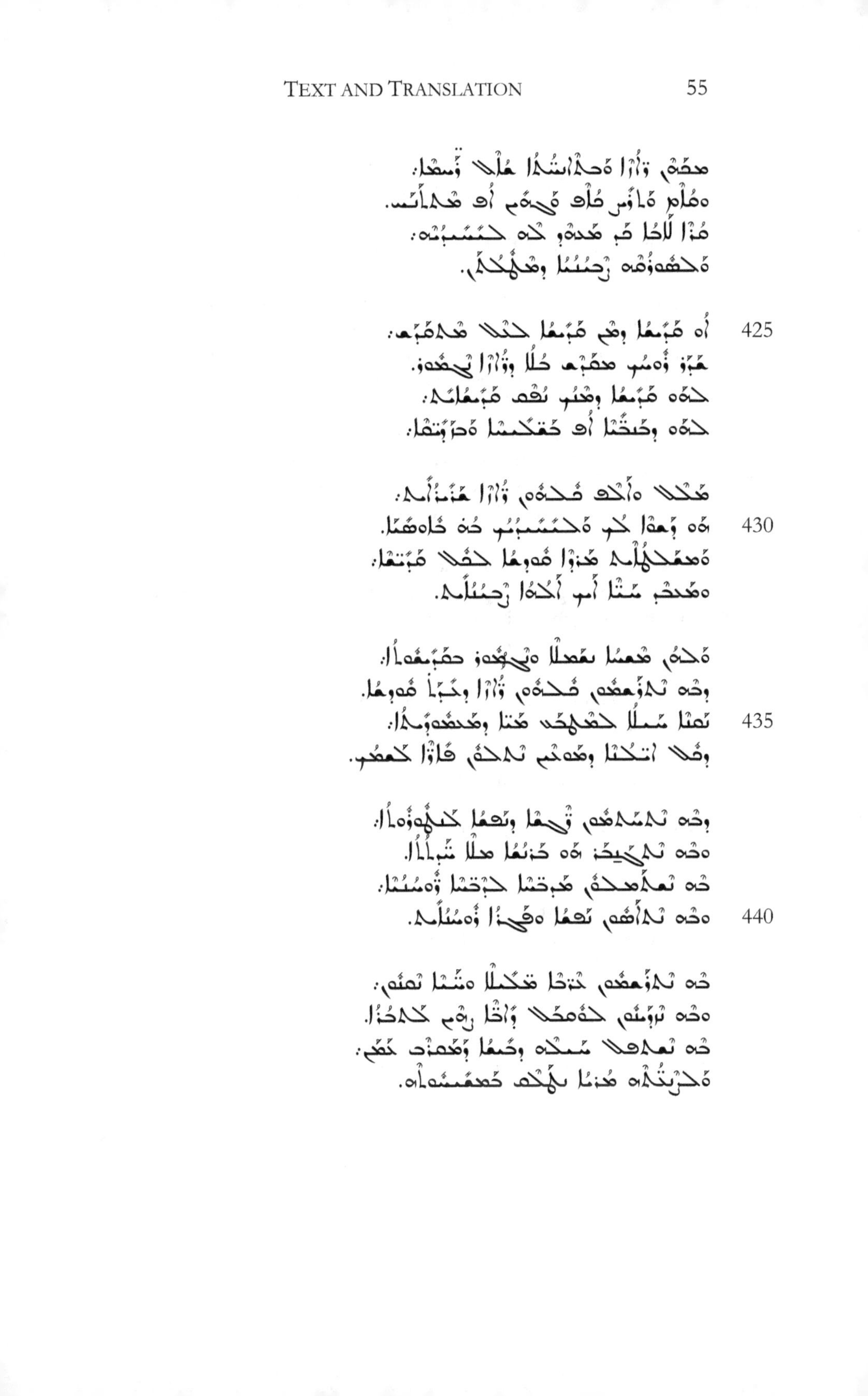

445 May the creation that became old with vanity, be renewed by it,
And may it be delivered by it from the slavery of the Accuser.
May Adam be dressed with the garment that he lost,
May the face of Eve that was ashamed be gladdened by it.

May the new sons be separated by it from the old ones,
450 May they be armed by it against the bow of the rulers.
With these hymns, he beseeches the Lord of the mysteries,
Whom he trusts to consecrate hidden things.

In mystery, he signs three crosses over the oil,
Signifying by it that the Trinity perfects the mysteries.
455 And when this liturgy is accomplished with perfection,
He ascends as (Christ did) on the Mount Olives to reveal Himself.[92]

Above the band of the apostles and disciples,
Christ the bridegroom ascended and He was lifted up to His Father.[93]
And therefore, in the middle of the Church, he shows himself,
460 As the Lord was exalted in the middle of the world.

He lifts up and lowers the gift as he holds it up in wonder,
As the Lord also extended His hands over the disciples.
He turns his face to the four directions to show,
That He has sent the mystery of His teaching to all quarters.[94]

465 In each direction he signs three crosses with wonder,
In order to announce the Trinity to the world without confusion.

An awesome cry that draws down mercy does he make in wonder,
And with extended hands, he draws down mercy on humanity.

---

[92] After the signing of the bottle as in the Eucharist, the bishop ascends the bema and extols the bottle towards the four sides. The commentary on Myron by George (ed. CONNOLLY) does not mention this rite.

[93] Cfr. Bar Kepha, *Myron*, ch.30. Acts. 1:9–11.

[94] Ibid., ch. 31–33.

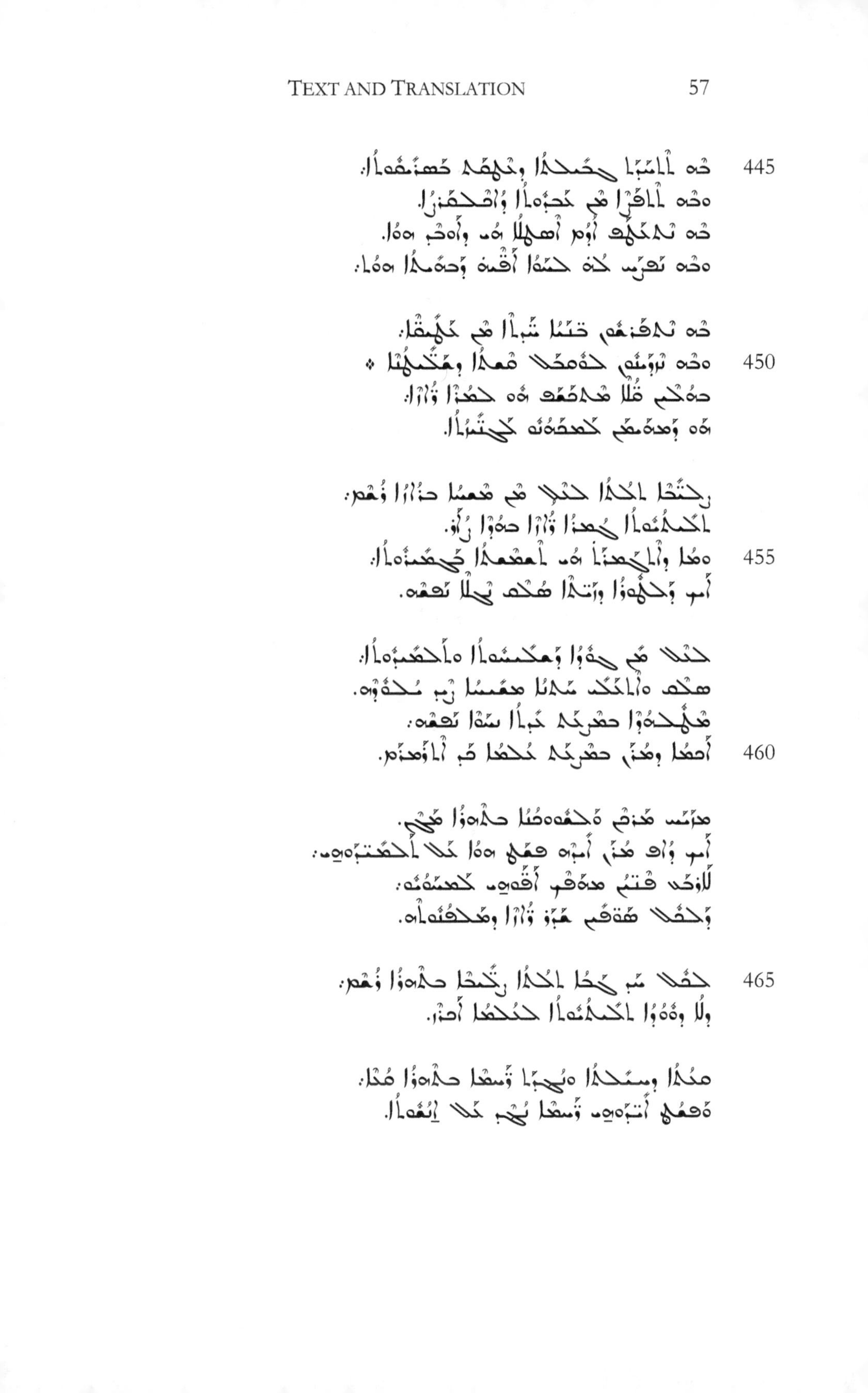

He returns to the Holy of Holies and enters with cheerfulness,
470 As our Lord does every day, He sanctifies us:
He is above magnificently in the bosom of His Father,
And below on earth, He always perfects and gives us delight.

'There He revealed a horn to David',[95] as he promised.
And lighted a lamp for his anointed one, as He promised.[96]
475 With great care, it [the Myron] is put away inside the Holy of Holies,
For the mystery of teaching ought to be guarded carefully.

(For) our Lord commanded: 'Do not give the holy things to the dogs,
Or casually throw pearls to the swine'.[97]
Let no one ever consecrate it without the bishop,
480 For, 'nobody says that Jesus is Lord, but in the Spirit'.[98]

No one ever does (any) good without Him,
For every gift of mercy is from Him alone.[99]
Only once we are signed, not a second time,
For the Lord is One, and therefore the faith is one.

485 Whoever sins after having received the seal of life,
Should have great compunction, for he has destroyed life.
And that is why baptism is sanctified,
So that it may truly be cleansing and purifying your faults.

By the death of the Son, descend to baptism and rise with Him,
490 For His death, burial and resurrection are represented there.
And since Our Lord remained in the tomb for three days,
Three times the baptized is immersed in the water.

---

[95] Ps. 131 (132):17.
[96] 1 Kgs. 11:36.
[97] Mt. 7:6.
[98] 1 Cor. 12:3.
[99] Cf. Jas. 1:17.

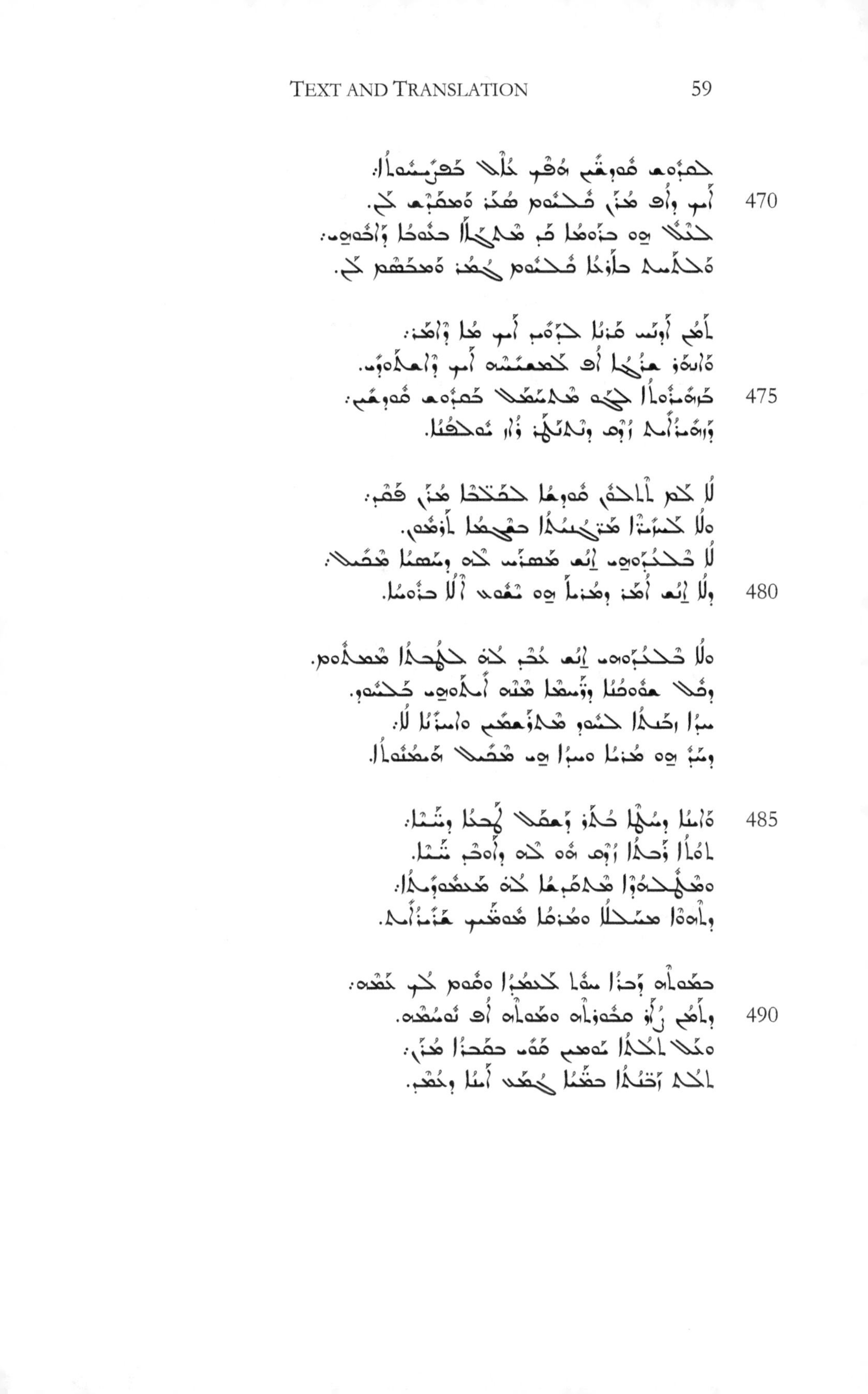

And in his ascent from the water, his resurrection is represented,[100]
And by His descent, He announced His death, when He was baptized.
495 We descend with Him in the baptismal font as if to a tomb,
And with Him, we ascend as He also (ascended) from the dead.[101]

The garment of death has been taken away from our members,
And behold, with the new garments of life, we are adorned.
The new man whom He had given us by creating us,
500 The transgression of the Law made him mortal and full of pains.

And for us, the Son of God descended for baptism,
So as to weave garments from the water to cloth us.
The clay that was worn out cannot be renewed, except with water,
And therefore, He opened His side to renew us[102].

505 Two sources, He made to flow to purify us,
He cleansed us with water and with His blood, He gave us absolution too.
The new Mother gives birth to spiritual children,
And the Table of Life nourishes them spiritually.

As there was a fight with Dragon in the water,
510 The fighter's body should be anointed with oil,
So that he slips away from the hands of the Enemy,[103]
Who has hidden himself in the water to ensnare us.

Oil is forever a great weapon to every winner,
None are crowned, except by the oil of anointing.
515 'He anointed my head with the holy oil', cried out the prophet,[104]
Give me to drink your wine, may I be inebriated with it, O Son of God!

---

[100] Commentary speaks of it as the sign of ascension, George, *Com.*, p. 14.
[101] Rom. 6:3.
[102] Jn. 19:34.
[103] Cfr. George, *Com.*, p. 14.
[104] Ps. 23:5.

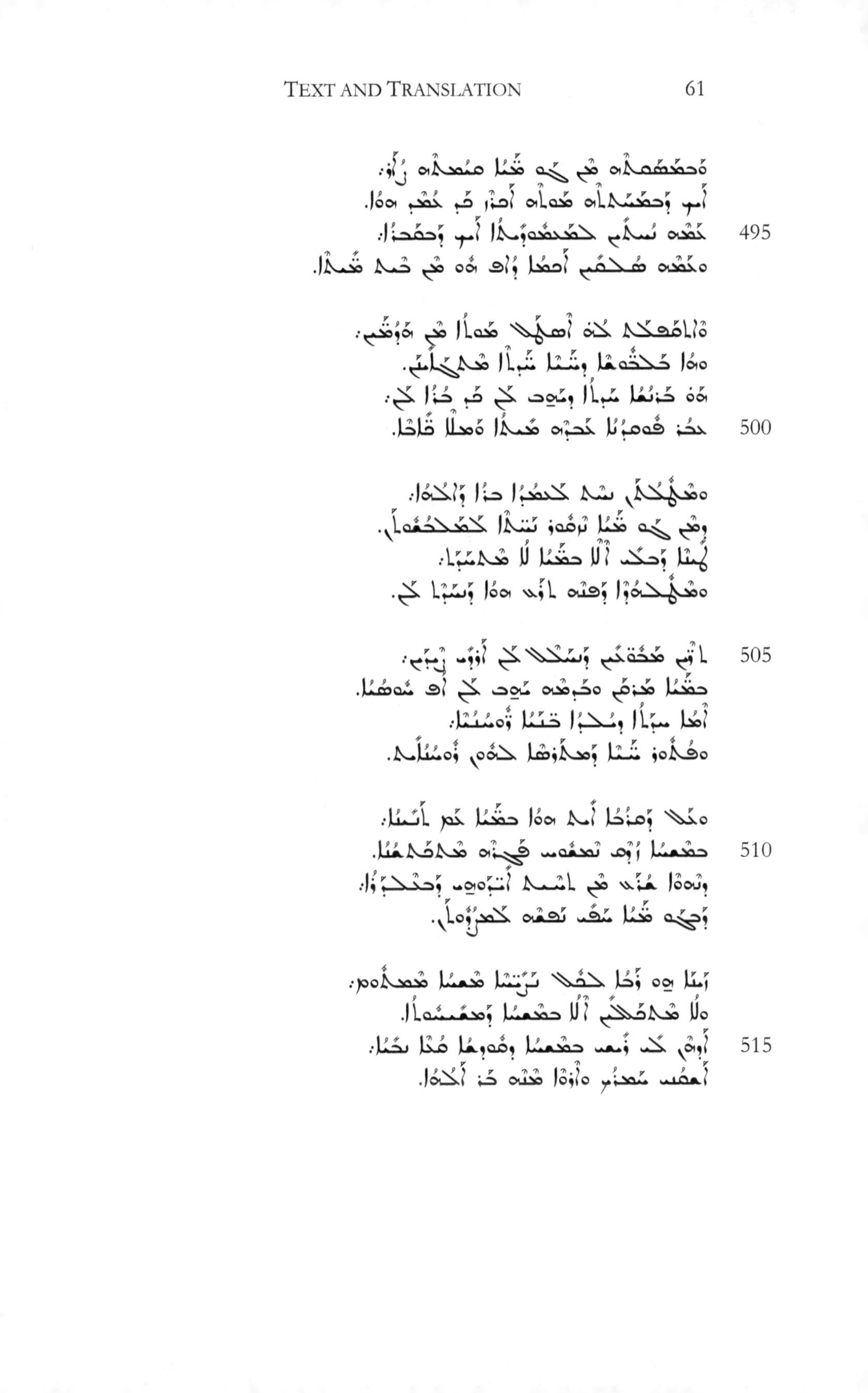

In the fatness of the oil He represented His anointing,
And through wine, he yearned for the living blood.
Through the revelation of the prophecy, the wondrous prophet
520 Perceived these mysteries, which he preached.

And therefore, the feast of the oil takes place first,
For it perfects the baptismal font with all kinds of gifts.

And he who descends is baptized, and ascends, made perfected and completed,
And then he approaches the Table full of life.

525 He who is not baptized, never ascends to the kingdom above,
Not even if he has every act of justice.
Listen to our Lord saying to Nicodemus:
Unless you turn to regeneration, you have no life'.[105]

Therefore he who eats His body, without being baptized in His name,
530 Eats (it) for judgement, condemnation and shame.
And he who drinks the Blood of the Lord and having no seal,
Has destroyed his soul voluntarily, according to the Law.

O unbeliever, receive his sign and then draw near,
To eat His Body and to drink His Blood with faith.
535 May your face joyful with the holy oil and may you will find delight in it,
Exulting and rejoicing, draw near with faith.

See that no deceit is in your heart when you draw near,
Lest you earn hanging like Judas.[106]
For he also received the Mysteries from the Son of God,
540 Since his heart was filled with deceit, he was exposed.

---

[105] Cfr. Jn. 3:5.
[106] Mt. 27:5.

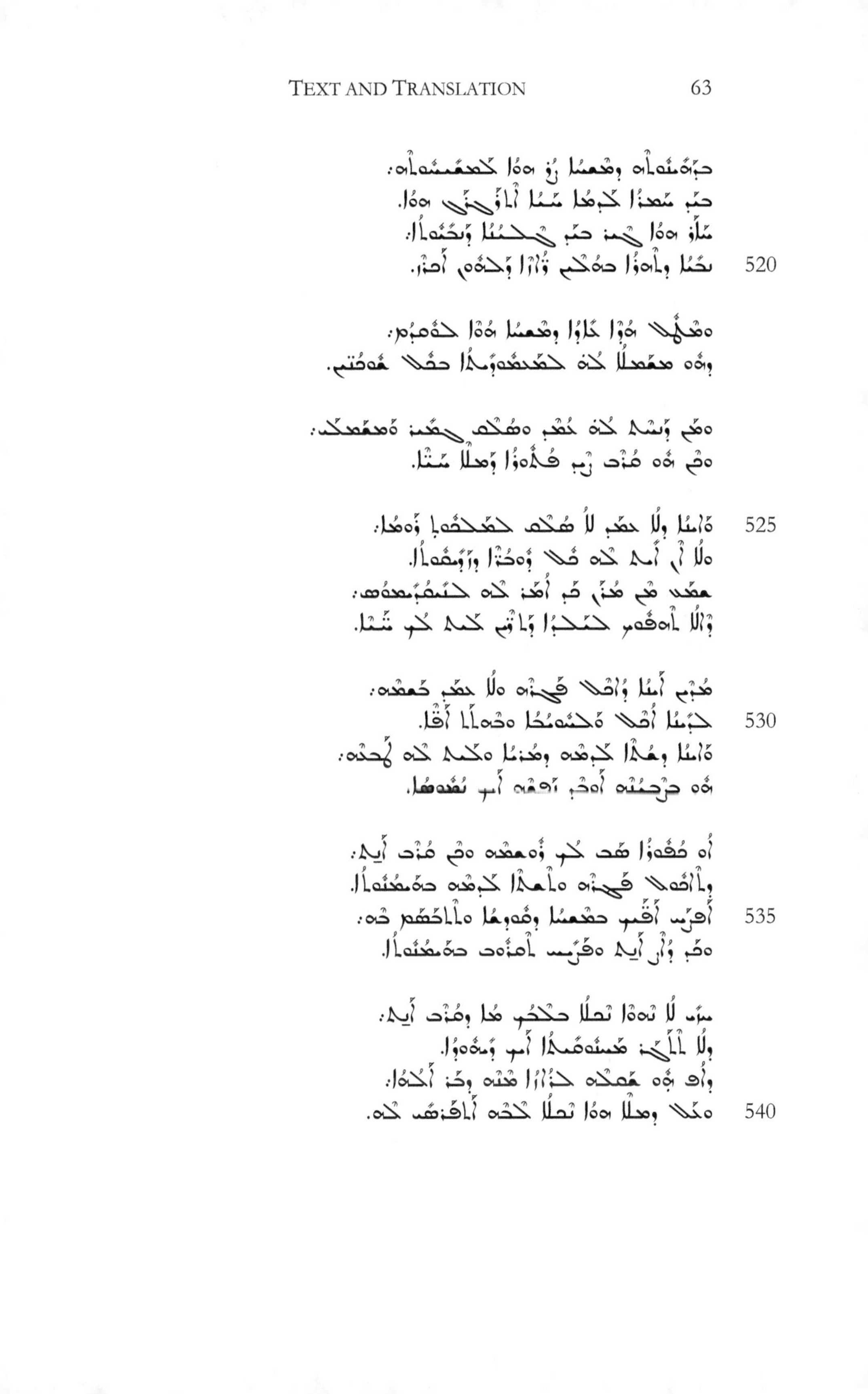

The Lord knows what is in your heart and it is revealed before Him,[107]
And according to your mind, He gives you reward for your faith.
And if you approach like Simon and like John,
You will rejoice with them, and you will delight in the Son of God.

545 And if you give a greeting with deceit like Judas,
Look at his reward, and if it pleases you, be like him!
That sinful woman took fine oil with her[108]
To the house of Simon, where He was reclining at table with His disciples.

She emptied the jar's content on the head of Jesus,[109]
550 And its fragrance filled the whole house and He was pleased with it.[110]

And since Judas was enslaved by avarice,
In his cunning he wanted to sell the oil.[111]

'Behold, the poor are always with you', said our Lord;[112]
'The women is depicting a mystery with the oil. Do not forbid her!'[113]
555 Look, the discerning (reader), how avarice and robbery,
Combined with audacity, withhold the mysteries and defraud truth.

And have the habit of depriving sinners of forgiveness:
Even if they take on the appearance of good, they bear deceit.
Who has deceived the Son of God like Judas?
560 And who hinders every good action like Satan?

---

[107] Acts. 1:24; 15:8.
[108] Lk. 7.
[109] Mt. 26:6–13; Mk. 14:3–9.
[110] Jn. 12:3.
[111] Jn. 12:5.
[112] Jn. 12:8.
[113] Jn. 12:7. Often the Syriac writers make use of elements drawn from the four Gospels to describe Christ's anointing.

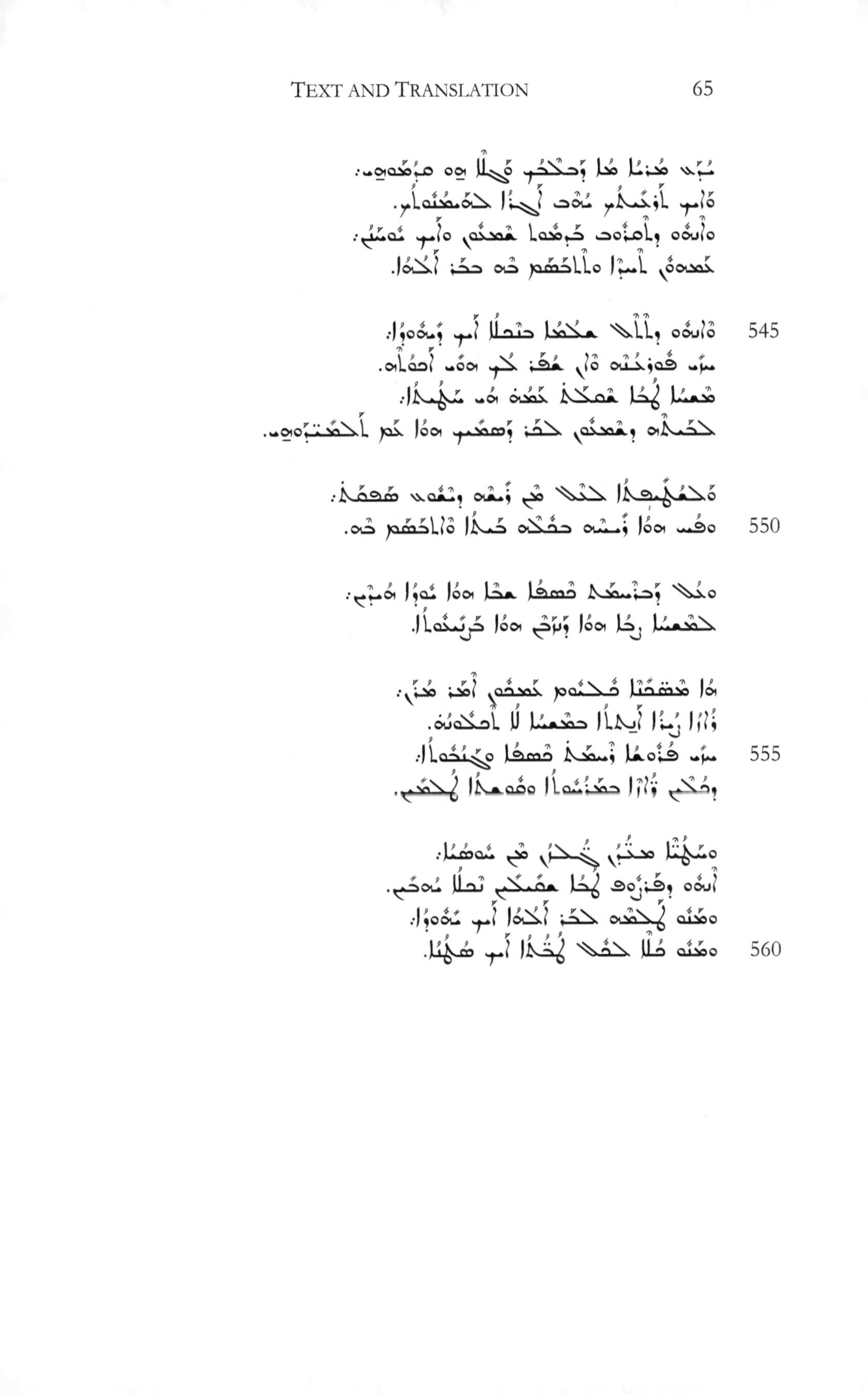

And who was praised for her audacity like the sinful woman?
And who has received absolution like her and sanctified by Him?
She has represented there the great figure of the Holy Church,
For she also committed adultery in idolatry and amassed debts.

565 Like the harlot, she took the perfumed oil and ran
And anointed the Son and He gave absolution because of her faith.
She let her tears flow and moistened His feet with (the tears) of her eyes.
She bowed down her head and wiped His feet with her hair.

Behold, she holds Him, embraces and caresses Him.[114]
570 She embraces Him and asks Him mercy for her children.
And if Satan, like Judas, wants to hinder her,
Behold our Lord is reclines like a hero to drive him away.

And he who, by his own will, inherited the hanging,
Behold by his freedom, he has chosen it, and also the Gehanna.
575 Blessed are you, O Church, for your soul desired His fragrance,
And with His oil, He had anointed your head when He betrothed you.

Blessed are you, O Church, for through the oil your cleansing was represented,
And by the jar of that harlot, your forgiveness was prefigured.

Blessed are you, O Church, who has poured your oil upon the Holy One,
580 And your face was made bright by His anointing, having (formerly) been downcast.

Blessed are you, O Church, for you have offered gifts for His entombment,
With the oil of myrrh whose fragrance wafts over creation.[115]

---

[114] Lk. 7:38.
[115] Cant. 1:3.

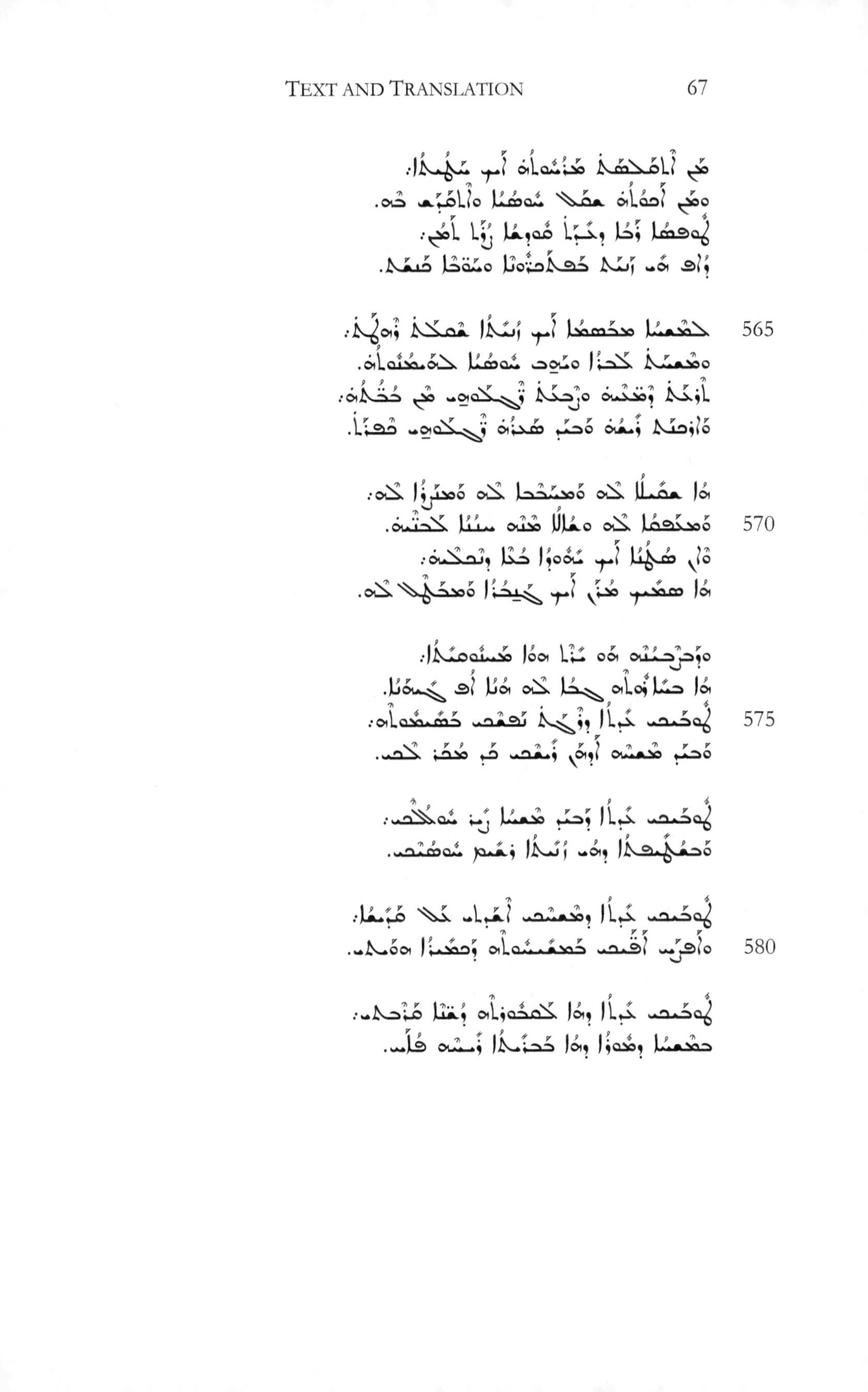

Blessed are you, O Church, for the Body of the Son gladdens your tents,
And your beauty is exalted like the sweet spices that give fragrance.

585 Blessed are you, O Church, for no sweet spice can be compared
To that plant who gave Himself to you, for He is heavenly.
Blessed are you, O Church, for behold the mystery of your memory is everywhere,
The nations rejoice, as He told you, when you perfumed Him.

Blessed are you, O Church, for (from being a) harlot, you have become holy,
590 And through the oil, the bridegroom has made you a virgin all at once.
Blessed are you, for the day of your barrenness has passed,
Behold, baptism gives birth to new children for you.

Blessed are you, O Church, for the Lord of the flock has given you His sign,
For everyone who comes to you will become a sheep by the anointing.
595 Blessed are you O Church, for all the mysteries of prophecy,
The Son of God has revealed and shown you on the day of His abasement.

Blessed are you O Church, for your mourning has passed, also your humiliation,
And behold the nations and the worlds thunder out in you with their cries of 'Holy'.
Cry out to your children to assemble from all sides,
600 For great and terrible is the mystery that is ministered today in you.

May the heaven rejoice and the earth exult on this day,
As well as the islands and the mountains, oceans and the air.
May the old be like the glorious olives in your courts,
And let them multiply the voice of their hymns to the Son of the Holy One.

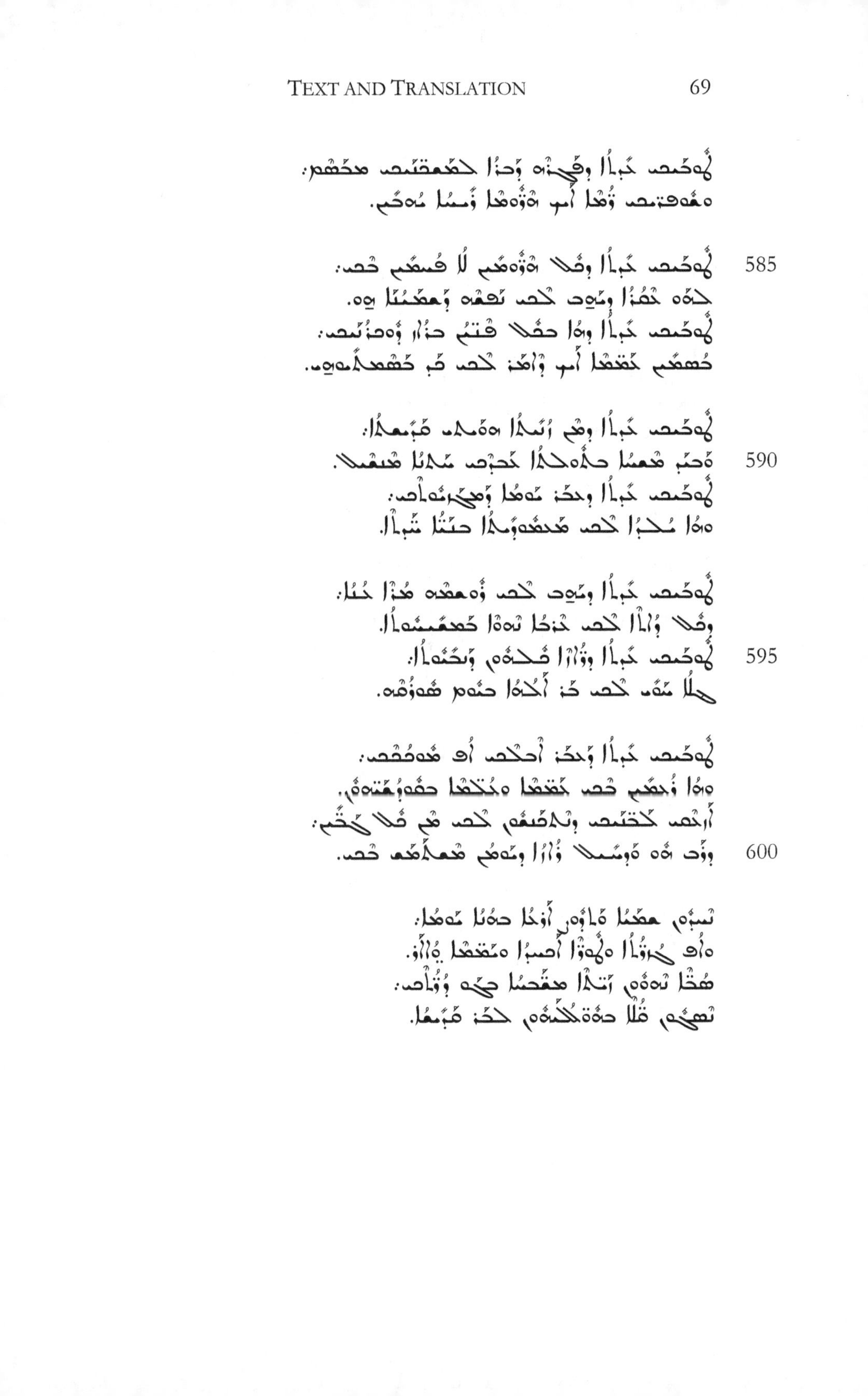

605 May the youth be like splendid palms with justice,[116]
And may they flourish even more than the cedars of Lebanon with their songs.[117]

May the children shout songs of praise with their hosannas,
May they exult in you, for pure is the sound of their simplicity.

May the virgins offer gifts with their lamps,[118]
610 Illumined by the excellence of their ways of life.
Let the chaste virgins, young men in their holy state,
Assemble, for they are beloved to the Son of the Holy One.

Let the married couples glorify Him who sanctifies union,
For she is the mother of all the righteous for all generations.
615 May the bereaved not abstain from praise today,
But let them give the sweet fruits of their tongues.

Let the barren exult, looking at the old priest,[119]
Who in holy fashion begot fruit in the barren womb.
'Let the brothers rejoice who will dwell together', sang David;[120]
620 He compared them to the oil that gladdens the head and the beard.

The beard of Aaron that descends with love on his collar,[121]
It is the Holy Spirit that the prophet here called oil.
Christ is the head upon which He descended, when He was baptized;
The beard is the Apostles, and those who confess are the collar.

625 Let the shepherd rejoice when he sees the entire flock,
Through the meadow of faith, he leads them all.
O pastors, raise the voice of your pipes!
Let the lambs exult with courage in your hymns.

---

[116] Cf Ps. 92:13.
[117] Cf. Ps. 92:12.
[118] Mt. 25:1–10
[119] Lk. 1:7; 24.
[120] Cfr. Ps. 132 (133):1.
[121] Ps. 132(133):2.

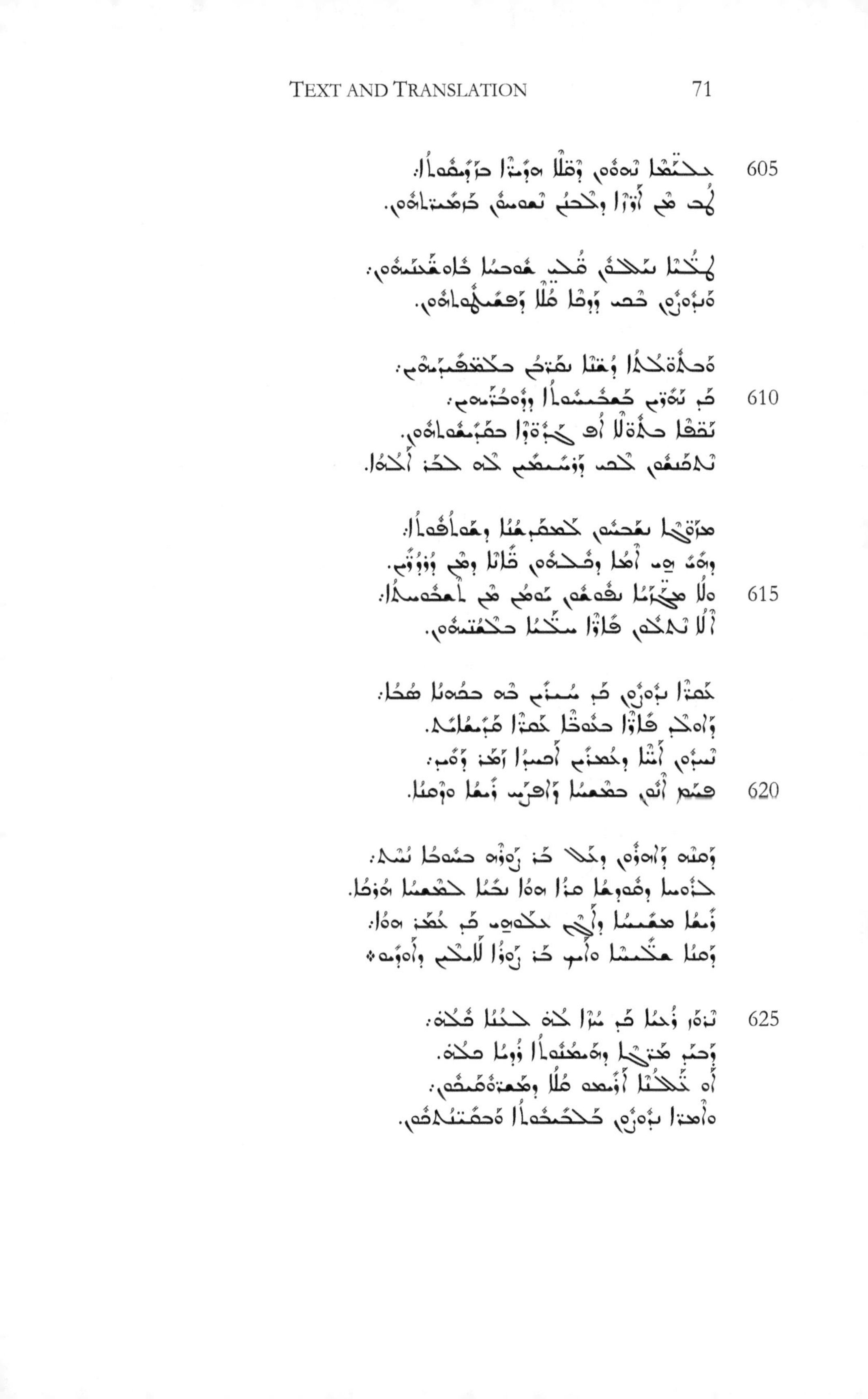

Let David awake, and with his sling, let him destroy uncircumcised (Goliath)![122]
630 For the Lord had chosen him and strengthened him by the holy oil.
Let Isaiah, son of Amoz also rejoice with us,
For it is him that the Lord anointed and sent for our healing.[123]

Let Adam rejoice, for behold his salvation has sprung up from the wood,
Because, it was from the tree that death sprung up in the beginning.

635 Let Noah the righteous rejoice and exult: behold the ark,
[The symbol of] the Church in which all sinners take refuge.

Let Jacob rejoice with the stone he anointed when he fled,[124]
For behold the chief-corner stone of the Church has been laid today.[125]
Let all the trees of the forests glorify the Son with us,
640 For, it is from them that He produced the oil that has healed the sores of Adam.[126]

Let the earth glorify, as well as the dragons that are in the depths,
The fire with (its) flames, and hails and snow with its whiteness.
The winds that blow, as well as the whirlwind (glorify) Him who made them,
And also the trees with their fruits and those who eat them.

645 Let the pools and springs and the reptiles in them glorify!
Let the birds exult, the flying creatures sing with their twittering.
Let the sun glorify our glorious Sun with its splendor!
Let the moon shine with all (its) many change;

---

[122] Cfr 1 Sam. 17:40; 49–50.
[123] Is. 61:1.
[124] Gen. 28:18–19.
[125] Mt. 21:42; 1 Pet 2:6.
[126] Cfr. *The Apocalypse of Moses* 9:3; 13:1–12; in E.M.C. QUINN, *Quest of Seth for the Oil of Life*, London, 1962.

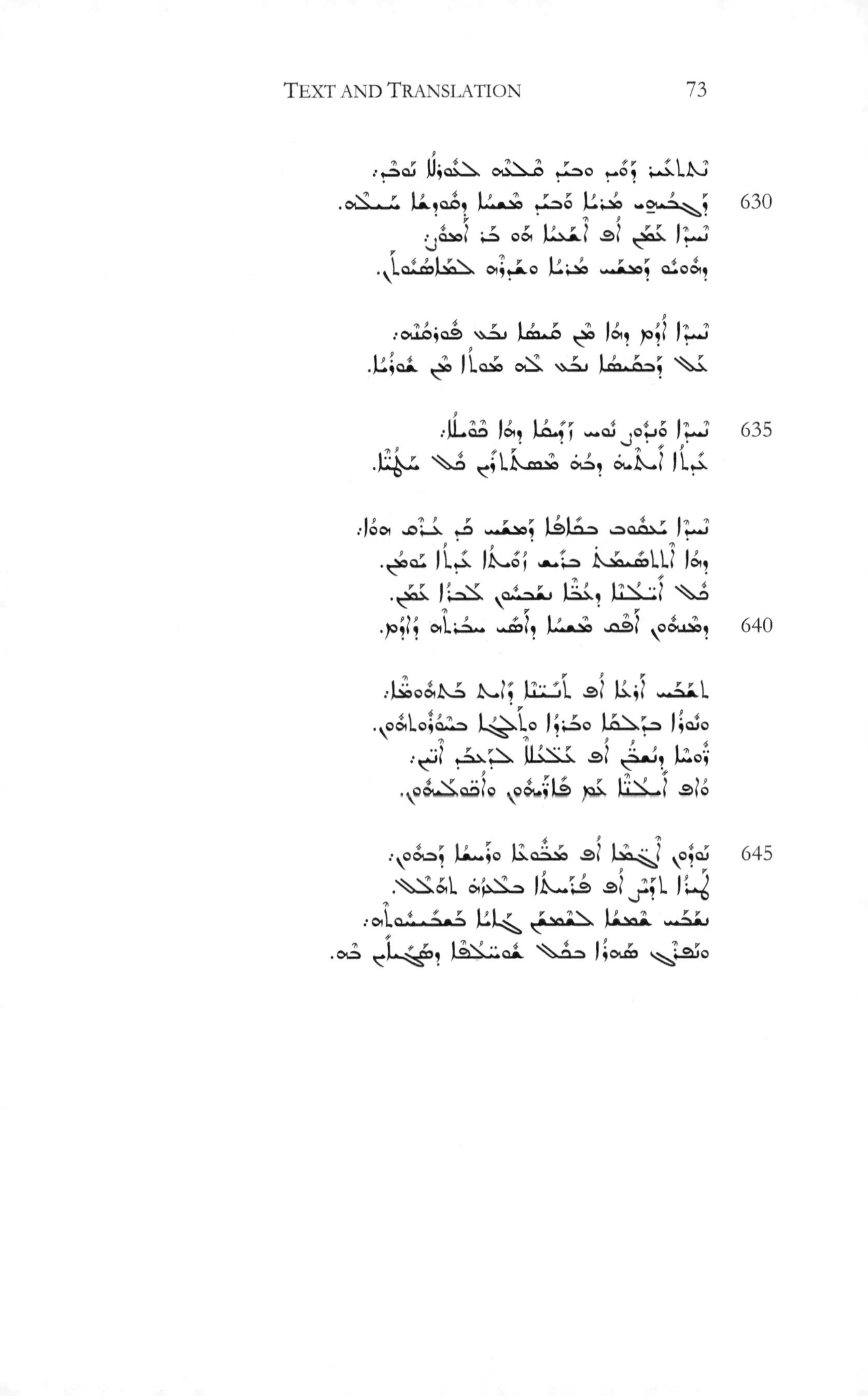

Let all the stars offer glorification with their appearances,
650 To the Son of the Holy One who receives every form of adoration from them.
Let the sky rejoice and all the waters that are above it,
In the Son who has shone forth among earthly beings and saved them.

Let the house of Gabriel raise the sound of its trumpets,
And let the house of Michael rejoice in (their) ranks with their canticles.
655 'Blessed is He, from His place', the Cherubim cry to the Son of the Holy One.[127]
For they see Him being sanctified among beings on earth.

With fear the Seraphim cry 'Holy, Holy',
To Him who was pleased to become a propitiation to His Father.
Let all the spirits in the heaven, with their exultation,
660 Praise the Son with loud voice on the day of His festival.

Fiery multitudes of flames with their hovering,
Let them honour the festival of the anointing of the Son f God.

The wheels of fire and all the ministers of spirit,
Let the sound of their praises thunder out with clarity.

665 'Holy, Holy, Holy, O Lord', cries the Church,
In the gathering of her children on this day, together with those above.
Holy is the Lord who sanctified me with His name and made me His own,
And through His oil, He has bound up my wounds and healed my sickness.

---

[127] Ez. 3:12.

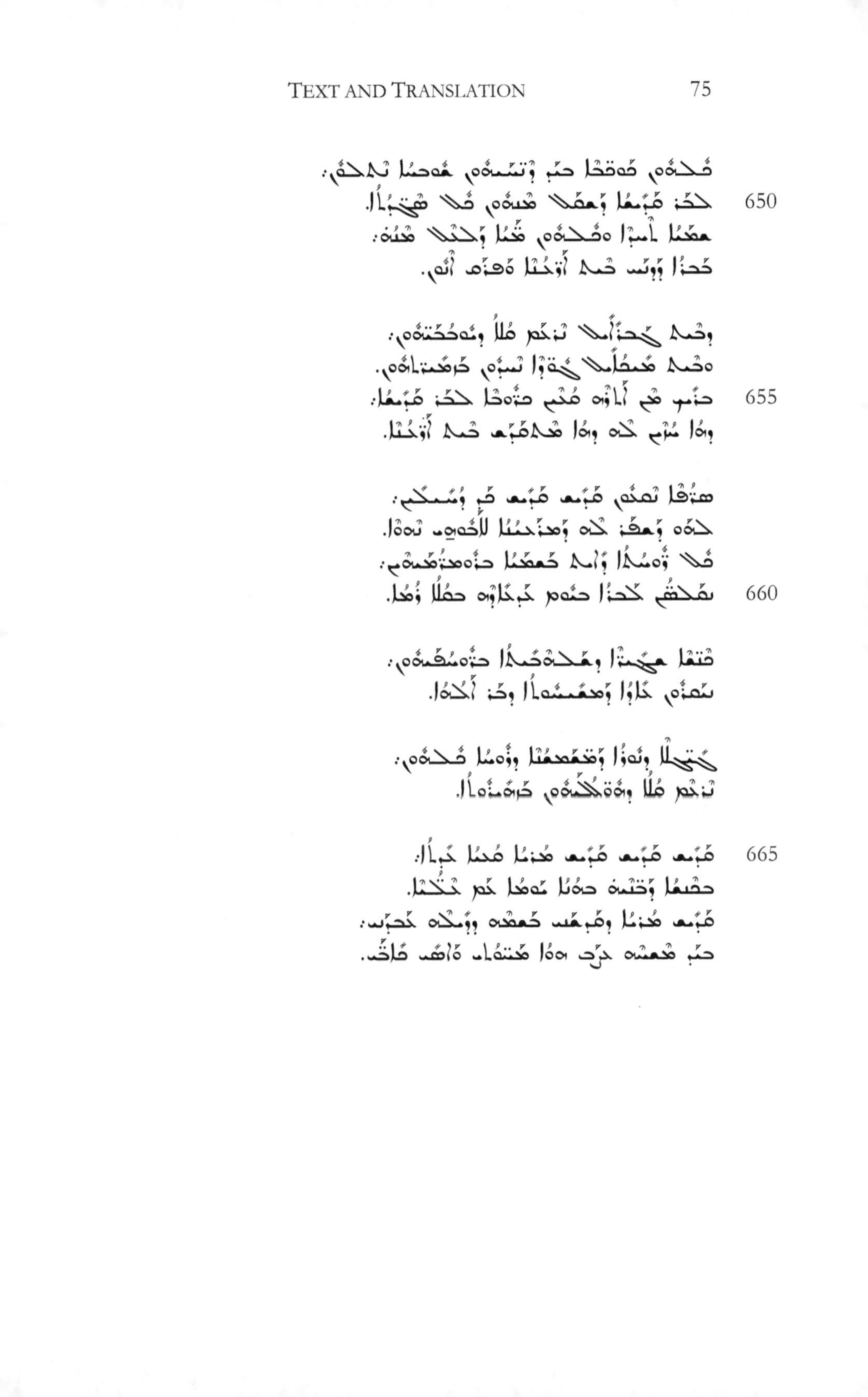

	Holy is the Lord, who gave me the oil through Elisha,
670	And repaid my debts and I became free and I was filled with radiance.[128]
	He is the Lord, cry out my children, to Him who sanctifies all,
	For He has made you His brothers in love and holiness.
	Holy is the Lord, cry out, all of you, in holy fashion
	To Him who, in His love, sanctified Himself for our sake.
675	Holy is the Lord who made us His temples for His hidden being,
	And He loves to dwell in a heart that is holy and full of beauty.
	Holy is the Lord who descended and saved us by His anointing,
	Even calling us 'christs' in His name, as it is written.[129]
	Holy is the Lord, from the fragrance of whose oil the impure flee,
680	And the demon does not endure the fragrance of His perfume.
	O Holy One, who is eternally holy with His Begetter,
	Be a protector to the holiness that you have given me, lest it be pillaged.
	Son of the Holy One, who has cleansed and sanctified me and greatly purifying me,
	Do not neglect me lest the Evil One pollutes my holiness.
685	O Hunter, who has drawn me to You by Your fragrance,
	May the evil not lie in wait for me, and seize me, for I am innocent;
	O Beauteous One, whose beauty and sweet voice has attracted me,
	Rebuke the hawk that dashes after me in its cunning;
	O You who emptied Yourself for my sake to gain me,[130]
690	Rescue me from the lion that roars and troubles me.[131]
	O Mighty One, who is always found by whoever invokes You,
	Hear me and answer me and let not iniquity dominate me.

---

[128] Cfr. 2 Kgs. 4:7.
[129] 1 Jn. 2:20.
[130] Cfr. Phil. 2:7.
[131] 1 Pet. 4:8.

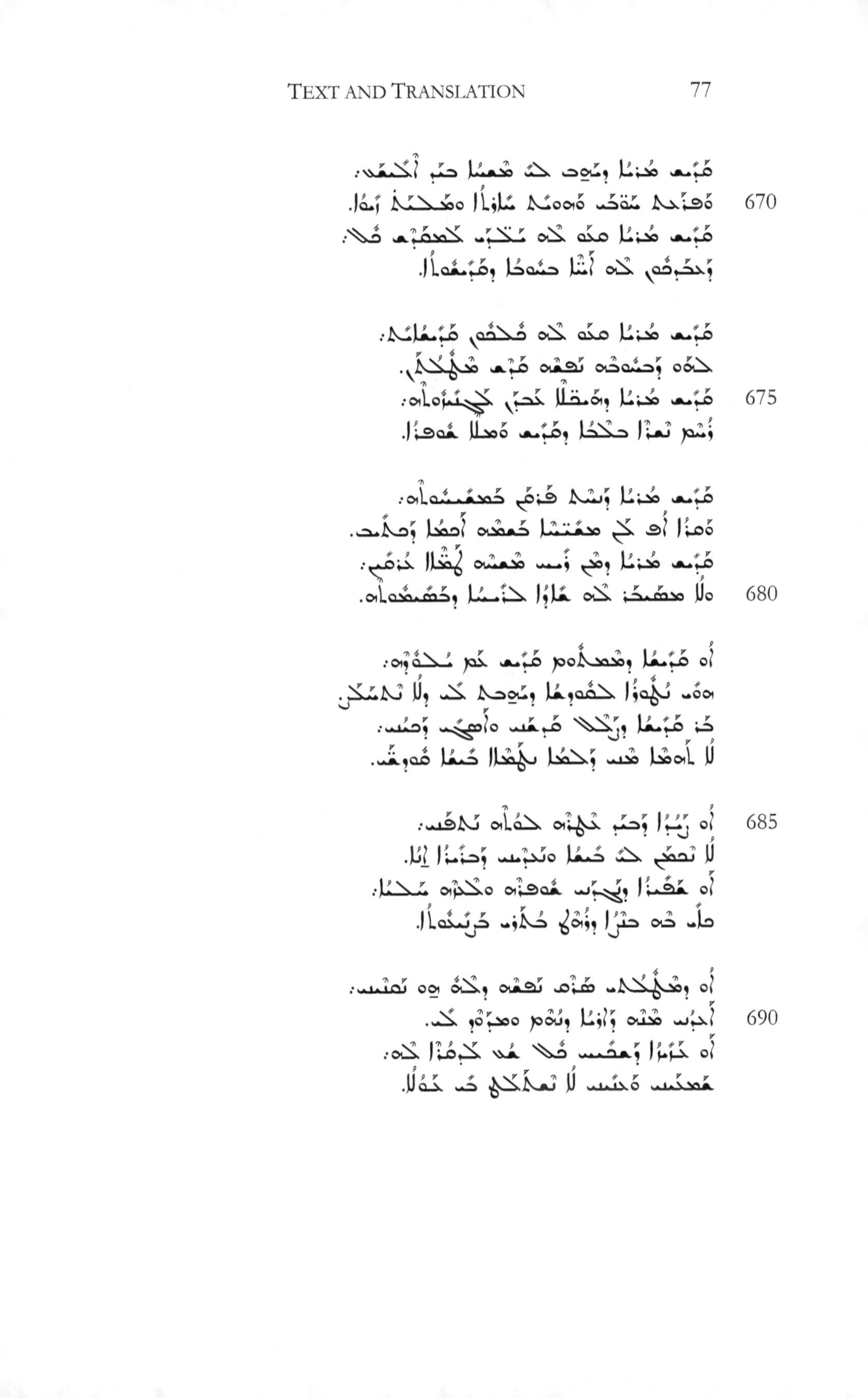

	You compared me to a lost sheep, as you delight in me,[132]
	May I never again perish from Your treasury, O Son of the Merciful!
695	In Your love urged me to imitate (serpent) in subtlety,[133]
	May I find strength in You, and hide my head from the persecutors!

You taught me to imitate dove in simplicity,[134]
In You may I be delivered bitter chase!
You taught me to call persistently like the widow,[135]
700   Do not delay (to answer) my supplication and request, lest I grow weary.

You have promised me that 'the bars of hell will not prevail against you',[136]
Do not neglect me, as I trust that Your word is firm, O Lord.
You promised me that, like Peter, You would build me,
But why have you abandoned me to be mocked by my enemies?

705   You have promised me (to put) the keys of the height and the depth in my hands,
Why do you not help me, when You saw my affliction?
You promised me that You would speak for me before the judges,[137]
But look, they are battering me with their blasphemies, while You bear with it.

You promised me the Kingdom on high and as being assured for me,
710   Do not bring upon me a testing for which I do not have the strength.
If my children committed faults before you, they are your (children too),
whether You chastise, or whether You forgive, or whether You pay no attention!

---

[132] Lk. 15:6.
[133] Cfr. Mt. 10:16.
[134] Ibid.
[135] Lk. 18:1–8.
[136] Mt. 16:18.
[137] Lk. 12:11–12.

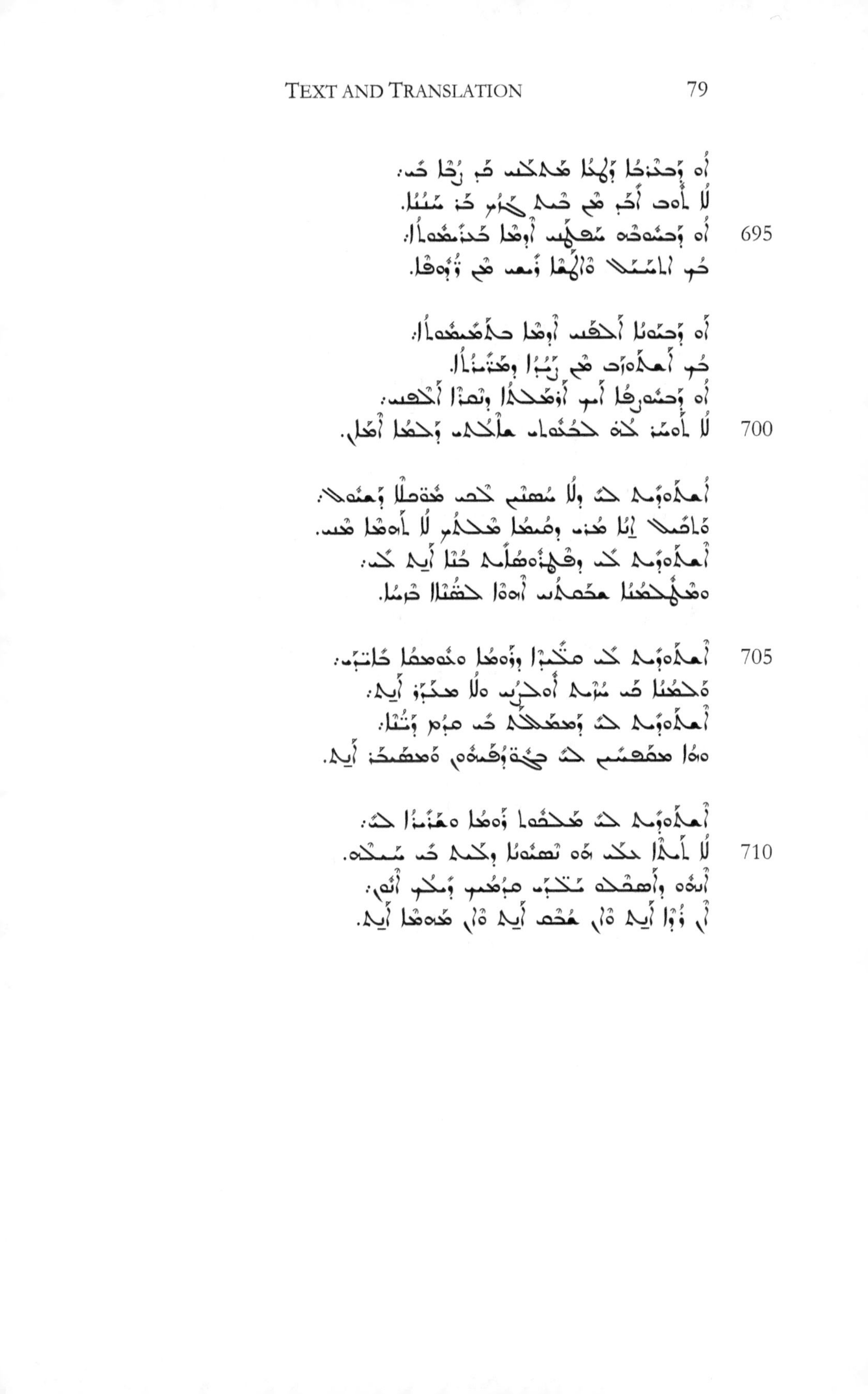

'Seven times and seventy times forgive and remit', as You have taught,[138]
May Your forgiveness abound even more, in accordance with Your greatness!
715 If they sin, being earth-born, in weakness,
Do You, as God, forgive and remit by Your grace!

If they backslide, being feeble with passions,
Do You, being mighty, strengthen them with watchful care!
If they succumb, being feeble, through laxity,
720 May Your great hope enthuse them with things to come.
If they are reviled[139] in Your great name by the envious,
Grant them (the grace) to possess a spirit that hastens toward the promises.
If they are insulted for Your sake in the assemblies,
Stand before them and give victory in their struggles.

725 If they are persecuted for Your love in (their) countries,
Go out with them and encourage them with Your promises.
If they are killed on account of hope in You, receive them,
And may their blood be sweet incense that pleases You.

If they are delivered to the flame by the wicked,
730 Be in their midst, as in the furnace with Ananiah and his friends![140]
And if they are handed over become food for wild animals,
Like Daniel among the Babylonians, deliver them![141]

If they are envied like the (three) beautiful men by the enemies,
By you, may they escape from the hands of every wicked person.
735 If justice chastises them for their sins,
May Your grace, O my Lord, quickly reach out and protect them!

---

[138] Mt. 18:22.
[139] Reading ܡܨܚܝܢ for ܡܨܚܢ.
[140] Dan. 3:20–30.
[141] Dan. 6:1–24.

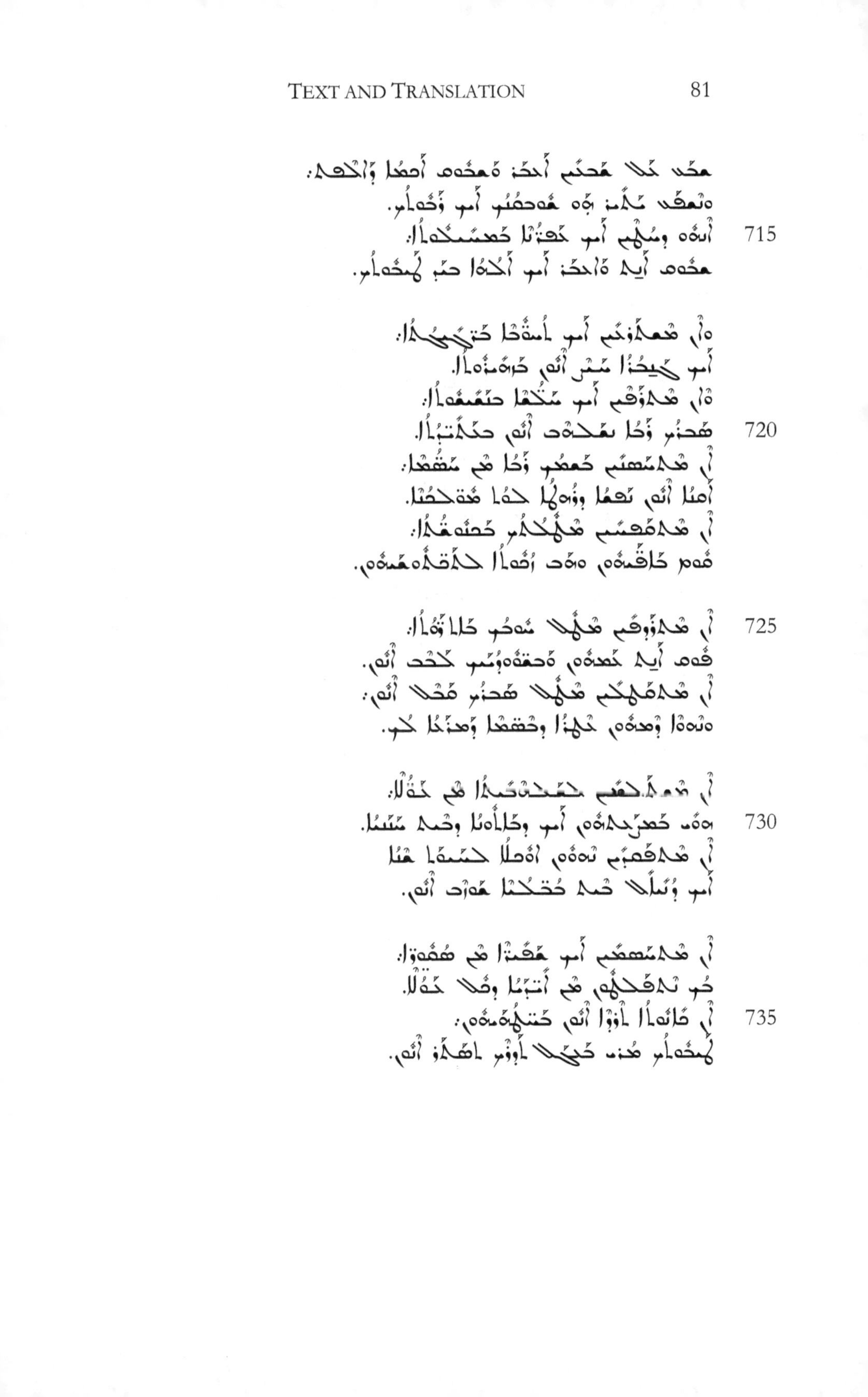

If they are ensnared by death that is ordained for everyone,
May Your living sign save them from Beliar.
The sword does not separate me from You, O Son of the Holy One,[142]
740 For the living words spring from You, as it is written.[143]

If the fire rises against me, it does not mitigate,
My desire for You, O Son of the Merciful, for You are fully life!
All torments will not cut off my love towards You,
For with You I have been freed from slavery to base things.

745 You endured insults and every kind of humiliation for me,
Yet, from being a harlot, You have made me virgin and chaste.
Even if I endure myriad of deaths for You,
I will not renounce Your truth, O Son of the Most High!

Protect my doors, lest all sorts of disputants enter through them,[144]
750 May those who love fighting and divisions be driven away from me!
May the children whom I gave birth assemble in me, for they are dear to me,
For through their mouths, I have learnt to confess the truth.

May all my offspring be protected in me in safely!
And let no stranger devising evil enter into me.
755 Establish my walls undisturbed by any denial,
And may Your Cross be a source of strength for my stones and roofs.

May Your mark act as a staff extending over my foundations,
May my every corner be protected closely by You!
May all choirs be arranged in due order by You
760 So as to give praise, girded with great power.

---

[142] Rom. 8:35; 38.
[143] Jn. 7:38.
[144] Cfr. Ps. 141:3.

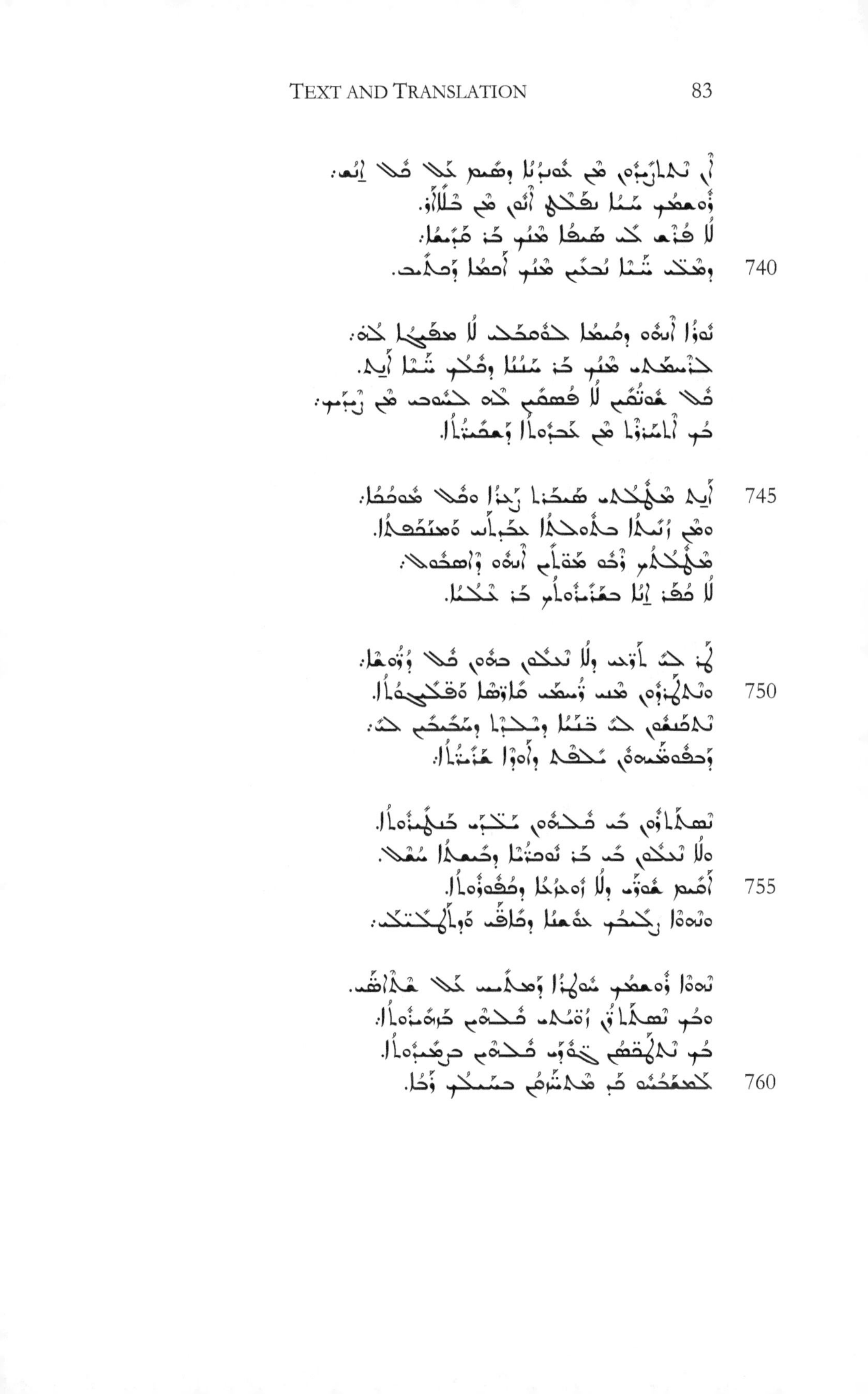

May all my offspring be armed by You against error,
May they be strengthened by You, to overthrow all heresies!
With noble mind, may they be fortified by You to fight,
Against Goliath the Accuser, even more so than David.

765 May they be encouraged by You, and with the sling of virtue,
May they fling stones of faith against the Evil One.[145]
May all the priests be anointed by You to minister
You with purity of heart and humility, O High Priest!

May my deacons be adorned by You to serve
770 Your great mystery blamelessly and diligently.
May all my offspring be incited by You to honor
Your great feast that illuminates minds and hearts.

May the leaders of my children, gathered together, be strengthened by You;
May all the sick be healed by You, O Good Physician!
775 May all who are tormented by Satan find relief in You!
May those who are captured by their enemies be delivered by You.

May the prisoners be released hastily by You!
May the needy be satisfied of their needs by You!
May the rich acquire life in You through their disbursements;
780 May all their treasures be stored up in You with confidence.
May plenty abound in You for the hungry and the poor,
By You, and for Your sake, may the naked be covered.
May the kings of the earth and the rulers be pacified by You!
By You, may they be persuaded to judge according to truth and rectitude.

785 May everyone who is lost from Your teaching be found out by You,
May all who are bruised be healed by You, O Medicine of Life!

---

[145] 1 Sam. 17:40–50.

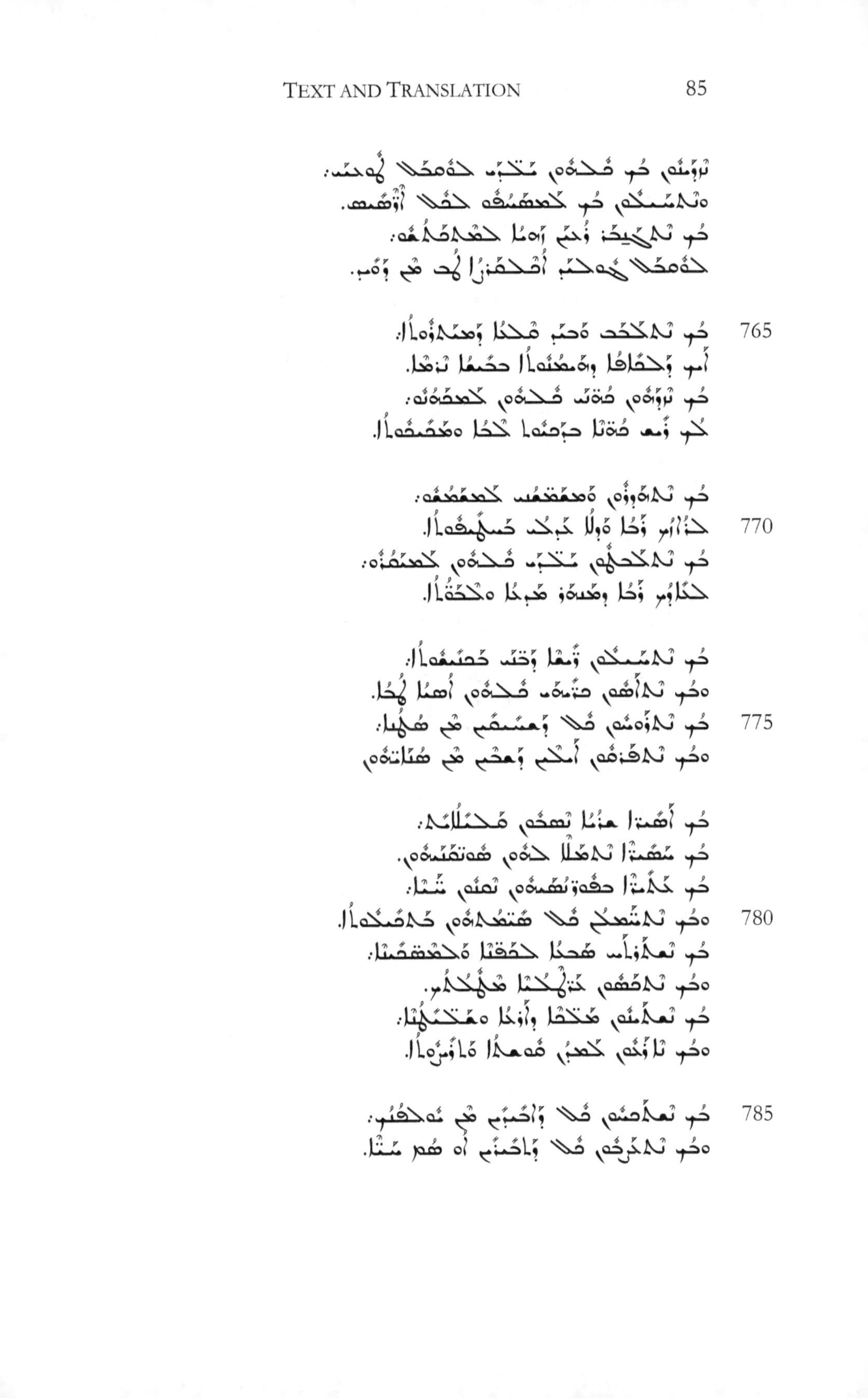

In You may everyone who takes his cross and follows You find courage;
In You may the beloved seal of virginity be strengthened.

You are the Lord of the orphans and the widows,
790 And also the one who sustains and nourishes all who are in need.
By You may all those in error be guided and may they turn to You;
By You may the wicked be changed and become good all of a sudden.

By You may we be delivered from the scourges and rods of wrath;
By You, may we be confirmed and in You may we live in faith!
795 By You may we flee from temptations and evil time;
By You may the crown of the year and the crops be blessed.[146]

In You, the fattened ox who died for us, may we find delight.[147]
In You may we arrive at an end full of justice!
With You may we travel to the place full of delights.
800 In You, may all the spirits of the departed find rest;

By You, may they be absolved from the defilement of their failings,
And may they go out to meet You when you come with great joy.
By You, may those who have consumed You be raised, O Merciful One;
In You may those who have drunk Your living blood be absolved.

805 By You, may all my offspring be gathered in Your bridal chamber of light,
And may they be with You, their lamps being alight[148].
With You, may we rejoice where the wise virgins dance;
With You, may we be refreshed in the blissful marriage feast in Your kingdom.

---

[146] Cfr. Ps. 62:12.
[147] Cf. Lk. 15:23.
[148] Mt. 25:1–10.

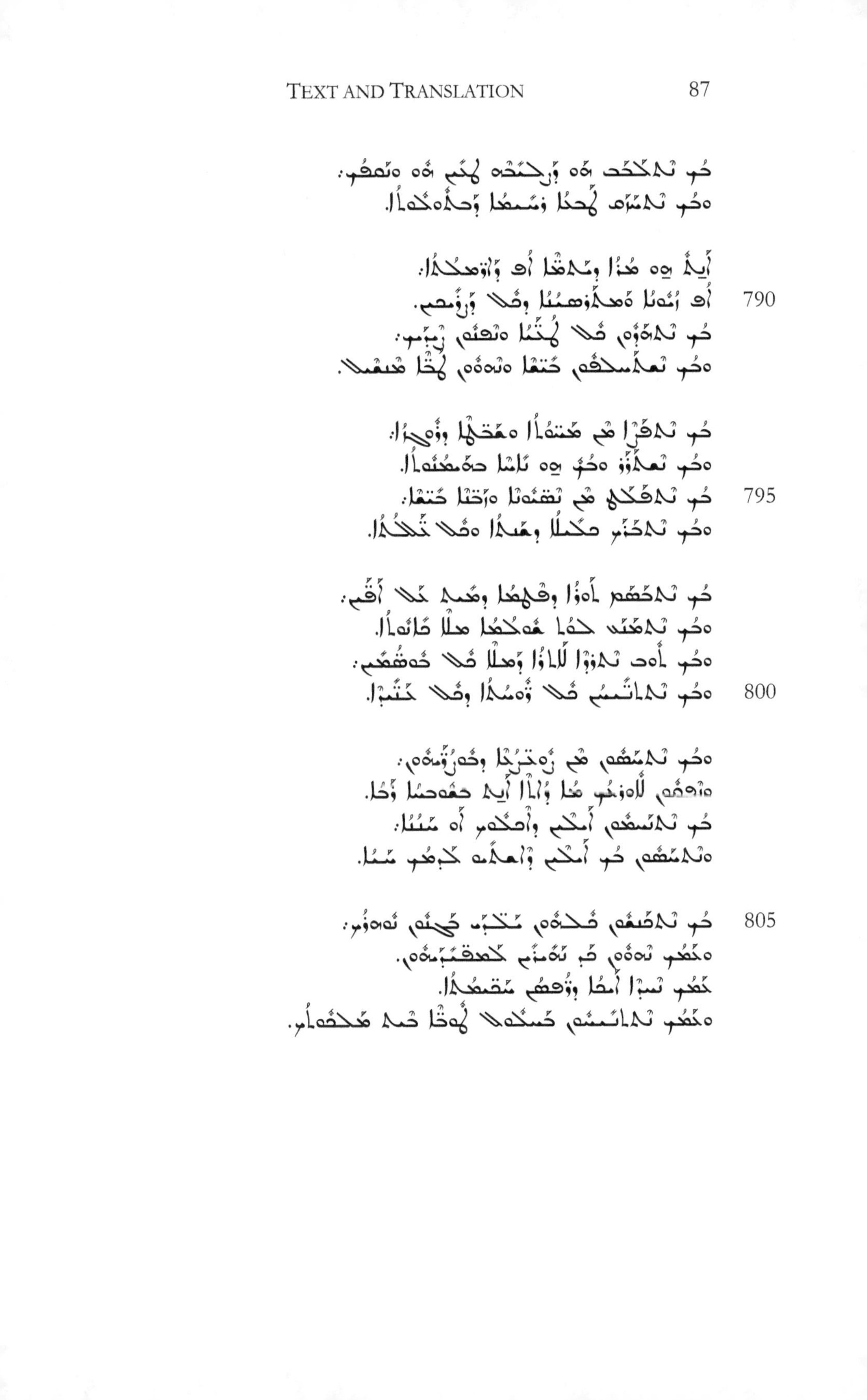

With You may we rejoice in the festival full of joy,
810 Where all kinds of praise thunders from the mouth of the saints.

There, may we all cry out with confidence and rejoicing,
'Blessed is the Holy One who has brought us to His festival with mercy'.

And there may we offer new praise with raised voice,
To You, Lord, and to Your Father and to Your Holy Spirit forever and ever! Amen.

END

ܥܡܟ ܢܗܘܪ ܒܗܘ ܓܒܠܬܘܐ ܡܠܐ ܟܘܫܦܐ:
ܐܝܟܐ ܕܪܫܡ ܡܠܠ ܐܡܫܘܚܬܐ ܒܦܘܡ ܩܕܝܫܐ.

ܐܡܪ ܗܠܠ ܫܒܚܢܘܬܐ ܐܦܐ ܒܚܕܘܬܐ ܢܪܢܡ:
ܒܪܝܟ ܩܕܝܫܐ ܕܒܓܒܠܬܘܗ ܒܪܚܡܐ ܐܬܟܠ.

ܘܐܡܪ ܢܫܡ ܫܘܒܚܐ ܚܕܬܐ ܒܦܘܡܐ ܙܡܪܐ:
ܠܟ ܡܪܝ ܘܠܐܒܘܟ ܘܠܪܘܚܩܘܕܫܐ ܠܥܠܡܝܢ ܐܡܝܢ܀

ܫܠܡ

Appendix

By Sebastian Brock

The manuscripts of the *mimro* on the Myron are divided in the attribution which they provide. The attribution to George is found in Vatican Syr. 117 (12th century), Paris Syr. 196 (14th century) and its copy, Paris Syr. 189; rather more commonly the *mimro* is attributed to Jacob, and this is to be found in (among the older manuscripts) Damascus, Syrian Orthodox Patriarchate 12/14 (11th century), 12/15 (12th century) and Vatican Syr. 118 (12th/13th century). On various grounds the poem can hardly be by Jacob, and it is easy to see how the attribution to George could have been be lost, since the *mimro* is regularly transmitted in manuscripts which are otherwise almost entirely devoted just to Jacob's *mimre*.

Ryssel's edition was based on Vatican Syr. 117. Since Damascus 12/14 is a century older, it has seemed worthwhile to indicate the main differences which it presents.

Main variant readings of Damascus Syr.Orth. Patr. 12/14 = D

(where D is supported by Paris syr. = P, in Ryssel's apparatus, this is also noted)

3	which ... humanity] whose strength filled the universe (= P)
4	resurrection] fragrance (cf. P)
5	filled ... intensity] which has given to the stinking world its fragrance (= P)
9	Delightful] Sweet (= P)
12	in giving praise] as I rejoice
17	Choice] Pure (= P)
20	so ... you] desired by You (= P)

22	may … me] and I will reveal them to those who are worthy of You
30	the harlot …. you] the sinful woman when she anointed You
31	I rejoicing … so] with courage
36	are … holy] become resplendent in (their) mission
42	role as tax collector] debt
51	Set now] May Your cross be
57	sanctified] emptied (= P)
67	omitted
70	at end D P add: And because they were not circumcised in the heart she drove them out
78	In your chamber they sprinkle cries of 'holy' from their mouths (= P)
81	humility] splendor
86	and … companions] truly
88	your face] his face (= P)
96	He has given you armour so that you may vanquish the rebel with its strength.
108	he … you] on your behalf
111	he … person] He, the Free-born, resided in the place of the departed.
112	To indicate His love, how He loved Adam, His image.
115	when it was closed] to the disciples
116	Although the doors were not open, He entered to reassure them
128	through his] through you (= P)
133	doubt … height.] have doubts over the humble things and exalted ones. [Against diphysites]
140	at the end D adds: The same on in might and strength, and in humility;
	For this reason He is also God enfleshed. (2nd line = P)
145	at the end D adds: So that I may speak, as one feeble, not being capable (cf. P)
147	Make … to] For Your name's sake may I (= P)
150	omitted in D and P
154	understood] perfected
155, 158	omitted in D and P
160	keep its distance] be found guilty
165	dove] lamb

166	bird of prey] wolf [read d'b' for db', 'bear']
179	investigation] doubting
180	puts on] sees
183	each day] with fire
192	he destroyed them] took them up (= P)
198	at the end D P add: And like a wise person he traded (P was diligent) and doubled them; For this reason he was entrusted with much.
201	bridal chamber of light] kingdom on high
204	mysteries] senses
208	That it will always] That everyone (= P)
212	By it he is illumined on the entire path of his activity.
216–217	D and P omit
219	at end D adds: Of knowledge and stood (there) naked; At the third hour the Lord of Adam entered the law-court
226	mysteries] beauties (= P)
227	they ... beginning] that all the just were symbolized by him.
228	In successive generations all forms of revelations (= P)
238	at the end D adds: And the Holy Spirit, and baptism, in a manifest mystery, a sign of love, an announcement of mercy and salvation, did the dove bear within the Ark to proclaim good news, just as the Holy Spirit rested on the Holy One in the form of a dove, and the world saw that He is the Son of God. (cf. P)
240	in symbolic fashion] luminously
252	the high ... sacrifice] the great mystery is established.
255–6	In the case of anyone who makes bold to make a similar compound That soul will die from the people in a bitter way. He commands that the one who depicts the mysteries should be hidden, For he thereby marks out the anointing of my beloved Son. (cf. P)
258	for my ... desire] it shall be preserved in a hidden mystery
270	To one person alone did he give the mystery to be enjoyed

271–2	D transposes the lines
273	Levite] Hebrew
278	anointed] marked (= P)
282	pure body] splendid head
283	that were hidden in him] luminously
284	For the river Jordan grew warm for Him at the Baptism
287	So with David as if this had actually happened.
295	pure Myron] fine myrrh (= P)
298	And in his childhood He filled him with wisdom and insight.
302	in truth] voluntarily
311–12	Priesthood, prophecy and royalty, For He is King, High Priest, and Lord of kings.
315–6	omitted (cf. P)
319	Come now and see the bishop clothed in the image of the Father, clothed in white, like light, in sanctity, resplendent, purified, trembling, quaking and full of fear. (= P)
326	at the end D P add: He empties out oil upon oil, mingling it carefully, For Divinity poured itself out over humanity: Hidden oil, since the Divinity is hidden, And oil that is (readily) found, for humanity is to be found every day.
333–5	D has the sequence 334, 335, 333
336	at the end D P add: Therefore take to yourself tears and suffering when you enter
338	omitted
344	Imitate Him who] At the meal He
353	nations of the earth] priests of the People
368	For with them Moses showed His type in the place of propitiation (= P)
374	the secrets] true things (= P)
377	choirs] mysteries
391	holiness] songs of praise
404	But our Sun leaves the west and proceeds; To the south He calls out 'Blow' [Cant 4:16!], as He gladly comes, for I have left behind me darkness and error. (cf. P)

APPENDIX

408	enters ... beatitude] and Warrior enters
428–9	omitted
430	at the end D adds: It is He who truly perfects all mysteries,
	Life-giving in divine and natural fashion.
433	this oil] the pure Myron
438	And may that person be renewed, full of joys
442, 444, 446	omitted (P omits 444 and 446)
449	new sons ... old ones] sons of the Church ... aliens
454	The number by which the Trinity is depicted.
457	Above ... and disciples] In the sight of ... He was raised up
458	The Son to the Father, with both sides gazing at Him
459	he shows himself] above the Bema
460	The mystery of the anointing ascends and manifests itself
465, 467	wonder] awe
470	does ... us] was raised up to His Begetter
481-2	He is distributed, with examination to those who are true,
	For the Lord is to be feared, and all disputers are unworthy of Him.
	For the purpose of its community (each) church takes some carefully,
	Just as in the case of the Manna, a measure for each, without any addition. (cf. P)
483	signed] baptized
486	There is no way that the Lord will be sacrificed (again) for him.
501	for us] because of it (= P)
508	them] us
515	the prophet] David
517	In the oil he depicted (baptismal) oil, which is full of life.
520	The Church first distributes the oil, and then the wine.
523	made perfect and completed] and is clothed in Myron
528	Unless ... regeneration] If you are not born of the Spirit
532	according to the Law] for ever.
539	For he too ate from the Table full of life.
553	Our Lord replied, Do not trouble the sage woman
554	Do not forbid her] in truth
555–8	omitted

565	the perfumed ... ran] faith and the oil
573–4	omitted
576	betrothed] anoints
583–4	omitted
590	Bridegroom] Mystery
600	ministered] consecrated
616	fruits] sounds
618	Who in old age begot the Voice who preceded the Word.
622	And the oil which descends over the head is the Holy Spirit
630	holy] good
637	when he fled] symbolically
638	at the end D P add: Let the mountains exult (P dance) like hinds in delight And let the hills too all leap like lambs.
640	at the end D adds: Let the sea rejoice for oil pacifies its surge, Let the pools and springs give thanks, along with the reptiles in them (= line 645)
642	whiteness] coldness
643	blow] give praise
645	omitted here (but see under 640)
646	at the end D adds: And kings of the earth, authorities and dominions. (cf. P)
651–2	omitted
658	propitiation to His Father] comprehensible to Dust [= humanity]
664	clarity] songs (= P)
671–2	Holy is the Lord: (when I was) weary and distressed He bound up my (wounds) and gave me relief in my distress; Holy is the Lord, who has made me fragrant with His oil, as with Myron, And when my scent wafts up He will bring me into his Chamber to rejoice. (cf. P)
684	at the end D adds: O Guardian, who stands wakeful for the watch, Do not abandon me lest the devil deceive me.
693	at the end D (cf. P) adds: On Your shoulders carry me so that I may ascend to Your Father's place –

APPENDIX

	You who sought out and found me in the lost coin.
695	In Your love] With the serpent (= P)
696	strength] wisdom (= P)
705–6	omitted
720	hope] compassion
727	killed ... received them] oppressed ... comfort them
729	wicked] persecutors (= P)
741	rise ... mitigate] roars mightily against me
742	It will not abate my love for You, O Son of the Merciful
743	cut off] separate (= P)
749	through them] into me (= P)
757	staff] measuring line (= P)
767	priests be anointed] chief priests be made resplendent
768	And all my priests, so as to consecrate in holiness
772	and hearts] of those who give You praise
773	leaders of] feeble among (= P)
775	May all who are afflicted find gentle relief in You;
	May all who are in grief find courage in You,
	And all who are afflicted by Satan be liberated by You.
	[cf. line 775]
786	O Medicine of Life] O Good Physician
789–90	May You strengthen the widow with love, for You are her husband;
	May the orphan find refuge in You, for You are the Father of orphans (cf. P)
794	we be ... faith] relief from (sources of) be strengthened
795	times] stirrings (= P)
802	omitted
806	be with You] rejoice in You
809	omitted
810	at the end D adds: Let us be there in the bridal chamber of light, full of delights
812	His festival with mercy] His Kingdom by grace.

INDEX OF BIBLICAL REFERENCES

Genesis		45:13	73, 87
2:7	187	45:15–16	76
8:11	233, 236	23:5	388, 515
27:27	4	24:7	407
28:18	239	36:10	211
28:18–19	637	62:12	796
Exodus		63:3	14
4:10	309	68:5	392
30:22–23	243	89:21	386
30:22–31	247	92:10	385
30:33	256	92:12	606
40:11	251–2	92:13	605
40:13	249	131(132):17	473
Deuteronomy		132(133):1	619
33:2	411	132(133):2	621
1 Samuel		140(141):3	51, 749
16:12	279	Song of Songs	
16:13	282	1:3	13, 582
17:40	629	1:12	5
17:40–50	766	Isaiah	
17:49–50	629	6:2	365
2 Samuel		14:12	393
6:5	384	54:2	413
1 Kings		61:1	632
3:12	298	Ezekiel	
11:36	474	3:12	655
2 Kings 4:7	670	10	367
9:2	299	Daniel	
Psalms		3:20–30	730
45:6	294	6:1–24	732
45:7	290	Habakkuk	
45:8	289	3:3	410–11
45:9	64	Malachi	
45:10–11	86	4:2	395
45:11	78, 83		

Matthew		10:16	163
2:11	91	11:9	210
3:16–17	93	12:3	550
4:2	95	12:5	552
7:6	478	12:7	554
9:7	105	12:8	553
9:9	41	13:5	344
10:16	695, 697	14:23	401
16:18	701	19:34	126, 504
16:19	129	20:19–23	115
18:22	713	20:25	117
20:3	217	20:26	115
20:3–4	218	20:27	117
21:7	101	Acts	
21:15	101	1:9–12	119, 458
24:42	638	1:24	541
25:1–10	609, 806	2:3	121
25:10	201	10:38	266
25:16	198	15:8	541
25:21	198, 200	Romans	
26:6–13	103, 549	6:3	496
27:5	538	8:35	739
Mark		8:38	739
14:3	5	1 Corinthians	
14:3–9	103, 549	12:3	480
14:15ff	109	2 Corinthians	
Luke		11:14	394
1:7	617	Philippians	
1:24	617	2:7	267, 689
7	547	Hebrews	
7:36–7	103	1:9	266
7:38	569	9:24	129
12:11–12	707	James	
15:6	693	1:17	482
15:23	797	1 Peter	
18:1–8	699	2:6	638
23:43–4	222	4:8	690
John		1 John	
3:5	528	2:20	678
7:38	740		

INDEX OF NAMES

Aaron	249, 621	John (Baptist)	310
Adam	185, 187, 219, 221, 447, 633, 640	John (Apostle)	543
		Judas (Iscariot)	538, 543, 551, 559, 571
Amoz	631	Judea	98
Arameans	45	Levite	248, 273
Babylonians	732	Matthew	41
Beliar	738	Michael	654
Bride	153	Moses	193, 243, 309, 338
Bridegroom	153		
Cherubim	367, 655	Myron	1, 13, 295, 352
Daniel	732		
David	73, 83, 283, 383, 473, 619, 629, 764	Nicodemus	527
		Noah	233, 635
		Olives, Mt of	119, 456
Dragon	509	Paradise	222
Egypt	195	Paul	146
Elisha	669	Peter	703
Eve	448	Phantasiasts	118
Gabriel	653	Pharan	410
Gehenna	574	Samuel	279
Golgotha	224	Satan	95, 560, 571
Goliath	764	Seraphim	365, 657
Hebrew	259	Simon	103, 548
Isaac	15	Simon (Apostle)	543
Isaiah	631	Solomon	298
Israel	195	Trinity	466
Jacob	239, 363	Yamshi	299
Jesse	61, 280, 372		

www.ingramcontent.com/pod-product-compliance
Lightning Source LLC
Chambersburg PA
CBHW070404240426
43661CB00056B/2530